| WINTER WOLVES |

To Charlene & Cleve

Earle Wacott

(Skip)

10 May 89

WINTER WOLVES

A NOVEL BY
Earle Wescott

YANKEE BOOKS

A DIVISION OF
YANKEE PUBLISHING INCORPORATED
DUBLIN, NEW HAMPSHIRE

Designed by Jill Shaffer

Yankee Publishing Incorporated
Dublin, New Hampshire 03444

First Edition
Copyright 1988 by Earle Wescott

Library of Congress Cataloging-in-Publication Data

Wescott, Earle, 1946-
Winter wolves.

I. Title.
PS3573.777W5   1988   813'.54   87-34644
ISBN 0-89909-160-1

For Sharon

Although other animals face downward and look at the ground, He made man look up towards the heavens.

Ovid, *Metamorphoses*

(Translation of the quotation on page 105.)

Sometimes, in reading a poem, the hairs will bristle at an apparently unpeopled and eventless scene described in it, if the elements bespeak her unseen presence clearly enough: for example, when owls hoot, the moon rides like a ship through scudding cloud, trees sway slowly together above a rushing waterfall, and a distant barking of dogs is heard; or when a peal of bells in frosty weather suddenly announces the birth of the New Year.

Robert Graves, *The White Goddess*

| WINTER WOLVES |

1 | THE old fellow was drunk and in trouble. He was un-
aware of the cold and of the snowy woods or what had
brought him through them from town. He put a hand over one
eye so there would be just one moon and squinted with the other
eye so the one moon would quit moving around up there.

He fell.

The soft snow of the woods had given way to the hard crust of
the flats and his boots flew up level with his eyes and he went
down hard on the seat of his pants. He sat for a while stunned and
unaware that the warmth of his body was leaching away through
the ice. The marshlands had crusted over all the way to the islands
so that spread before him was a broad moonlit plane dazzling
with ice crystals.

"Remarkably boo'ful," he said, taking care with the first word
and letting the second go to hell.

He rolled over on his hands and knees and saw a dark stain on
the crust where he had been sitting. He put his nose to it and
sniffed. A look of grave concern crossed his face. He reached

around to his back pocket and pulled out the neck and a few pieces of glass held together by the stickum on the green label of a pint of Wolfschmidt vodka. The rest was loose glass jingling like change in his pocket. He had cut himself, but his worry was over the loss of vodka, not the loss of blood.

He got to his feet and went on, not back through the woods toward town but across the flats where the islands stood out in the distance. There was no breeze. It was too cold for one, and that made him feel warm. He sang.

> *K-K-K-Katy,*
> *K-K-K-Katy,*
> *I'll be waiting at the*
> *K-K-K-Kitchen door.*

The caw of a raven answered from the island woods. Peculiar. He had never heard a raven at night before.

It took a while getting across the marsh to the salt-water channel. The night was so clear the islands seemed just a step ahead, but they were many steps — and a fall or two — ahead. He was winded by the time he arrived and, because he had broken his bottle, sobered. Not drastically sobered. He still had enough alcohol in his blood to render a temperate man unconscious, but sober enough to realize he had no business being where he was.

"How'd you reckon on getting over anyhow, you old fool — swim?" He looked across into the sheltering spruce boughs. "Where'd you leave that skiff?" He searched along the bank where the slick crust went down to the black water. He didn't find a boat. Instead he came to an ice jam that had stuck in the narrows to make a bridge.

"K-K-K-Katy!"

He tested the ice, placing a wary toe, then the full weight of his foot on the span. He inched his way out on jagged floes that had been welded by freezing mists and undercut by the tide. He gave her a bounce, with an ear cocked for the sound of give. Up came his boots and down he went on the very center of the span. Not a crack — except maybe in his own old bones. The bridge was solid as iron.

He crawled the rest of the way. Once on the island he got up and brushed the frost from his pant legs and gazed down the white scythe of shore toward the crooked black mass of a distant building. He smelled smoke, stale smoke from a fire that had been out a while. Maybe somebody had been down to the boathouse.

He started for it and had covered some distance before noticing there were two black outlines, not one. He put a hand over one eye so there would be one building and squinted so it would behave the way a building was supposed to. The trick didn't work this time. With one eye or two there were still two objects and one of them was getting bigger. Might be the man who built the fire. He watched it come closer.

Hell, no man was built that low to the ground. No man trotted with such ease over glare ice. Then by moonlight he got a look at its snout and he turned and ran for his life. He slipped and fell and got up and ran and his ears were full of the erratic thunder of a bad heart and the wheeze of worse lungs. There were terrible sounds from the thing that was gaining on him.

The ice bridge. What made him think he'd be safe if he made it? He looked to see how far and saw a blood-red glow seeping from the snow around the bridge. Barring the way was another of those shaggy horrors, this one sitting on its haunches looking across to the mainland. Suddenly it glanced back and smiled at him with a mouthful of star-bright teeth.

I   I   I   I

The dreamer awoke to full consciousness, as sometimes happens after a nightmare. He propped himself on his elbows and stared into the darkness. The clock said 4:01. He did not try to go back to sleep. Nightmares had a way of picking up where they left off. He hadn't had one in a while, a sign that he had hoped meant he was on the mend. This one left him discouraged, like a relapse. Sometimes remembering a bad dream helped to shake it off. He tried recalling some detail that would bring back another, and so on, until he had the whole picture. He could not find a thing to start with. He came across parts of other dreams — a soft, blue California sky and the smell of hot tar and eucalyptus trees at Rancho La Brae, his grandfather's rocking chair rocking with nobody in it — but nothing from the nightmare.

Maybe he hadn't had such a nightmare. Maybe he only dreamed he had.

2

WHEN his editor said the word *wolves,* Fran Thomas thought of an assembly line. He thought of the exhibit of prehistoric dire wolf skulls at the Page Museum in Los Angeles, dozens of them with only minor variation in size and state of preservation, and each stained an oily mahogany by the tar of the pits. It had been then, a year before, that Fran first thought of the assembly line — how brutally mechanistic nature really was, stamping out skullcaps like brass shell casings in a wartime munitions plant. The sameness of those massive bony hemispheres had shaken him, because he saw that the idea of human individuality was a mutation, an abomination in the eyes of nature.

"Probably nothing to this wolf angle," Ray Neville said, his own balding scalp under bright lights not unlike the others Fran had been thinking about. "But check it out anyway."

"Not much of a story without it," Fran said.

Ray detected something like sarcasm in Fran's voice. He didn't like it for two reasons. First, he was editor, and if anybody was going to be sarcastic, he was. And second, he was an Oklahoma country boy who had made good up north, and he had spent the past twenty years battling superior, smart-ass Yankees.

"I suppose out there in California a man's death was no big deal," he said.

"It was when it was murder," Fran came back.

Another thing Ray could not abide was giving anybody the last word. "I don't know if this is murder or not but it's yours." He started to say something else but thought the better of it. He let himself cool off. Fran could tell that was what he was doing because the flush in the tips of his ears lowered like mercury in a thermometer.

"It's the salt I put on those fries at lunch," he said. "Pumps me up."

"Poison," Fran agreed. It wasn't so much that he knew how to rub people the wrong way. He just had trouble rubbing Ray the right way.

Ray sighed. "All the good things are poison."

Fran left the editor's cubicle and went back to his desk. There were still a few minutes to deadline and the newsroom was a madhouse. Fran had gotten his story in early. Maybe that was why Ray had given him the new assignment, that and his experience on a big city paper. He looked over his notes. Edna Sergeant, local correspondent for Steel Harbor, had phoned in the death report of Samuel Comstock, sixty-two, of that town. Comstock was found that morning in the nearby Channel Islands wilderness area by a man named Woodrow Wilson Parker. Although cause of death was determined as heart failure, the body had been disfigured by scratches and bites, and Parker claimed that Comstock was killed by wolves.

Steel Harbor. The Channel Islands. Names Fran had been familiar with as a boy. The oldest memories were so often the freshest. They brought back the smells and sounds and purity of childhood. But this afternoon there was another, less identifiable feeling mixed in with the others, something more recent and not at all pure.

He telephoned Edna Sergeant. Steel Harbor was half an hour from Riverston, longer under icy road conditions, and he did not want to drive down at night. In winter these little seacoast towns rolled up the streets after dark.

"This is Fran from the *Republic*," he said when she answered. "I'm calling about the story you filed today."

"Tragic, wasn't it?" she said happily.

"I don't know. I called to find out."

She became suspicious. "Ray is going to use it, isn't he?"

"It'll play tomorrow."

"Page one?"

"Inside."

"Darn, I've never made page one. I had high hopes for this one."

"That's what I wanted to talk to you about. Ray's asked me to do a follow-up."

"Well, there are hordes of Comstocks in these parts and excellent attendance is expected at the funeral. It'll be closed casket. Albert says a showing is out of the question. He says there's only so much even he can do." Albert was Edna Sergeant's husband. He ran Steel Harbor's one funeral home, the source of most of Edna's stories.

Fran asked if she had seen the body.

"I did not. And I wanted to, too."

"Besides your husband, who did?"

"Let me see. Woody Parker — he found Sam as you probably know — and Mal Boulding, our chief of police — he's half the entire force for that matter — and Dr. Tagen. Poor Dr. Tagen. Albert says this has been too much for him. He's old as Methuselah."

Fran interrupted. He said he'd like to come down in the morning and talk to her and then the others. One question couldn't wait until morning.

"What's this business about wolves?"

"It's Woody Parker's business."

"Any truth to it?"

"Mal Boulding says a pack of dogs must have defiled poor Sam's remains. Albert and Dr. Tagen concur."

"What does Parker say about that?"

"Woody Parker is a queer man," she said, her tone of voice changing from chatty to exasperated. "You'll find that out for yourself."

3

FRAN said his good nights and put on his fleece-lined leather flight jacket. He had bought it in L.A. one brisk afternoon out of a nostalgia for changing seasons. He hadn't been able to wear it half a dozen times out there; now he had to wear it every day. He went downstairs, zipped up, and stepped out on the sidewalk. After the close, smoky newsroom, the night air was so cold his first breath was like inhaling something noxious — sulfur dioxide or tear gas — and he felt a withering ache in his lungs. Soon the cold pureness was making him giddy. It was still January and people were already saying it was Maine's coldest winter in half a century. Young TV weathermen made up like actors talked glibly of the coming ice age.

On the way home he stopped at Jimmy's Market. Jimmy charged more than the supermarkets but Fran liked to go there. It was the Maine of his childhood again, a place that was getting harder and harder to find. He liked the clutter of merchandise and the smell of cheese and sawdust and the meat cooler, about the size of a coffin, with the white enamel top that vibrated to the touch. He gazed through the glass at the tiny wilderness of cracked ice and red meat. Jimmy kept his ice immaculate, the mark of a good butcher. His apron on the other hand looked like it had been used in a ritual slaughter.

"What's for supper, Mr. Thomas?" Jimmy said, waddling behind the cooler.

Fran asked for some expert advice.

"Tell you what I'm taking home for mine. The flank steak. Eats like butter and not a speck of waste." Jimmy's hand appeared in the glass case and fetched a cut of meat on waxed paper for Fran's inspection before weighing. On the way to the cash register Fran picked up a cold six-pack of Pabst Blue Ribbon.

"They force-feed beer to beef critters over there in Jap-an, you know," Jimmy said as he rang up the purchase.

Fran said he didn't know and Jimmy looked surprised.

"Read it in the *'Public.'*"

Fran admitted he didn't always read everything in the newspaper. This was news to Jimmy.

"In last week. Awful informative."

"You a Riverston native, Jimmy?"

"All my life."

"Ever hear anything about wolves coming down from Canada in the winter?"

"Can't say I have."

"Suppose a man's body were found ripped up in the woods. What animal would you suspect?"

Jimmy exercised his imagination. His fat little face screwed up and he licked his lips. "Bear," he said with conviction. "Tidewater fella got himself cuffed up bad a couple years back. Shot a blackie sow in the rump with a .22 and she turned on him." Pause. "That was in the *'Public,* too."

Wolves, dogs, and now bears. Fran had a funny feeling about this story, and not the kind of funny that makes you laugh.

He left the brightly lit market and crossed the dark street to his apartment. Maine cities had not gotten over being small towns. There were few street lights off the main drags. Many of the apartment houses were formerly private homes. Fran rented a loft in such a house, which meant that he lived on the third floor of a two-and-a-half-story building. The nice thing about living on the second-and-a-half floor in winter was that he didn't have to worry about the heat. That precious commodity rose through the drafty house and warmed his rooms on its way to the sky. But not tonight. Tonight it was so cold there was frost on the inside of the windows.

Fran had chosen the apartment for the same reason he went to Jimmy's and had come back to Maine. He felt safe here.

He went into the bathroom and turned the shower on hot. The air was icy against his nakedness when he took off his clothes. He stepped into the steaming stall and felt warm for the first time all day. He stood motionless and let the pelting water beat the cold from his bones. He looked down at his body. It looked its age. It hadn't until recently. In California it had been slim and tanned, now it was skinny and pale. It had been kicking around for thirty-five years and had accumulated a history in its scars and irregularities. For instance, there was a groove on the ring finger of his left hand where his wedding band had turned the skin the color of sea-spoiled copper. Susan said that gold was hypo-allergenic (her word) and that what he was really allergic to was marriage.

Jimmy knew his meat. The flank steak was grained and juicy without waste, and Fran ate it with a sliced tomato and a can of beer. He did not have a second. In the old days he might have. In the old days he might have had all six and a pack of cigarettes to keep them company. He thought of his old self as a different person entirely, a careless young man who had assumed that the elasticity and boundless nervous energy of youth would see him through. It hadn't. The collapse of his nerves had hit with the impact of a heart attack. At first that's what he thought had happened to him. There followed a succession of doctors, each more specialized and expensive than the last. His regular man, an internist, diagnosed exhaustion. An endocrinologist suspected a hyperthyroid condition. A consulting cardiologist was partial to angina pectoris. When the neurologist suggested neuralgia, a discouraged and skeptical Fran figured that if he had consulted a veterinarian the diagnosis would have been distemper.

Meanwhile, the attacks continued: the spasms and dread by day, the evil dreams at night. He found relief only in quitting things — booze, cigarettes, coffee, the *Herald,* Los Angeles, Susan. Actually she had left him, but she tried to make him think it was as much his doing as hers. They were self-actualizing (another of her words) in different directions. They'd both be happier in the long run. Maybe she was right in the instinctive way women so often are in matters of the heart. Maybe she was giving him leave to leave, something he never would have done on his own. He had the archaic notion that marriage was for keeps and that divorce was less a matter of admitting you had made a mistake than of breaking your word.

In the past few months since his return to Maine he had begun joining things again — the *Republic,* even his long-neglected church. He had tried confession.

"Bless me, Father, for I have sinned. It has been eighteen years since my last confession. These are my sins."

A sigh from the other side of the partition. "All eighteen years' worth, my son?"

"I'll stick to the headlines."

4

FRAN drove his Volkswagen down the rutted snowpack of Tidewater Road. He passed the noisy paper mill and entered the quiet woodlands that separated Riverston and Steel Harbor. To his right, along a swath cleared through the spruce forest for power lines, he saw the big river, boiling cold, the icy gray water steaming into the icier air.

The relationship between Steel Harbor and Riverston was gravitational, that of a small moon trapped in orbit around a dominant planet. Steel Harbor people — lobstermen, farmers, mill hands, and their families — had their babies and bought their groceries in Riverston, while Riverston people owned the choicest ocean front, kept summer cottages, and moored their boats in Steel Harbor. As natives liked to point out, Riverston Dump was technically on Town of Steel Harbor property, and that was a pretty fair indication of the way the city treated the town in other respects as well.

The center of town was laid out in a T, with the marina pier at the end of the main drag on the harbor. The Widow's Walk Inn, the hodgepodge of offices called the Town Building, and a row of fine old New England houses arched gracefully over the hill to the crossroads where Sergeant's Funeral Home, itself a converted mansion, lay directly across the intersection. Some of the houses needed a coat of paint, but not the funeral home. Dying was one thing Steel Harbor people didn't have to go to Riverston to do.

"Please come in," the gentleman said, gently, reassuringly.

Fran saw that he was being mistaken for a bereaved relation and introduced himself.

"And I'm Albert Sergeant," the man said, as if he knew who Fran was all the time. He ushered Fran inside and called upstairs, "Edna, your fellow scribe is here."

Mrs. Sergeant came down like Joan Crawford, with a swing to her shoulders instead of her hips. A pair of glasses hung at her bosom on a pearl eyeglass chain, and her smile was full of pearly teeth. "I know we've met before," she said to Fran, allowing her husband to hand her down the last few steps.

"At the office Christmas party," Fran said.

"That's right. You're the new reporter Ray Neville introduced." She sighed in recollection. "That man should not drink. And his smoking!"

Mr. Sergeant shook his head solemnly. "Livers and lungs. I'd like to have a nickel for every case I've seen."

"I should think, dear, you've been recompensed a slightly larger sum than that," said his wife, with a wink at Fran.

Mr. Sergeant laughed pleasantly enough but used the word *scribe* again. He said he'd leave them alone so they could get on with their work.

"And so you can get on with yours?" Fran said.

"Well, yes."

"Any chance of my seeing Comstock's body?"

Mr. Sergeant pulled at the skin of his wrists as if he were adjusting a pair of white gloves. "The casket has been sealed and cannot be opened without the family's permission."

"I understand that the body was mutilated to the point there wasn't much you could do."

A look passed between the Sergeants.

"Dr. Tagen will fill you in on all the gory details," Edna said, taking Fran by the arm and steering him toward a pair of open French doors. "Coffee and muffins? I hope you like blueberry. Sally made them up fresh this morning. The berries are frozen, alas."

"Excellent nonetheless. I had two myself," said Mr. Sergeant, as if his having had two rather than one established forever the merits of Sally's muffins.

"Don't mind Albert," Edna said as she led Fran through a suite of chilly showing rooms to a sunny kitchen. "I don't."

Fran asked if there were any new developments on the story.

"Mal Boulding and some of the others have been searching the islands since yesterday. To no avail, so far as I know. Take this one on top. It's just riddled with berries."

"The islands — that's where Parker found the body."

"Woody, yes."

"Who claims wolves were responsible for the mutilation."

"He claims they outright killed Sam. Cream and sugar?"

Fran asked where he could find Parker.

"It won't be easy tracking that man down. He lives in a shack out near where it happened. Even if you did find him he wouldn't talk to you."

"He must share your husband's prejudice against scribes."

She gave him an arch look. "Sam Comstock was our town drunk. Woody Parker is our hermit. Your best bet is Caroline Parker, his niece. She's the only one who can handle him."

Where could he find her?

"You'll have to be careful there, too. Caroline keeps her own counsel. Not shy exactly. Moody. Good head on her shoulders, though. She manages the inn, took over after her father died." Pause and a grimace, as if she had bitten into a sour berry. "Her mother's a different kettle of cod. She could use some of Caroline's reserve." Her expression became philosophical. "But then that's the way it so often is, isn't it, when the mother was a beauty in her youth and the daughter's plain? Let me pour you some hot."

Full of muffins and coffee, Fran found his way from the funeral home to the doctor's house. It was another great white clapboard Greek Revival affair, more like a tomb than a house. The side annex looked like it might be a doctor's office so he went around and knocked. He was greeted by an uproar of howls and growls and scratching, then a man's voice and loud, harmless blows like those delivered by a rolled-up newspaper.

"For heaven's sake, whoever you are, go round front."

Fran did, and waited.

"Come in, come in now."

He turned the knob and stepped into a deep, gloomy hall, made all the darker by the blinding sunshine on the snow outside. Before his eyes could adjust, his nose sorted out three distinct smells: disinfectant, dogs, and age.

"Dr. Tagen?" he said to the figure taking shape from the shadows.

"I'm Tagen."

Fran identified himself.

"Thomas? Any relation to the Havenport Thomases?"

"That's right."

The old doctor's mouth twisted like a baby's, frowning and smiling in turns. He must have been eighty, tall but stooped, with hairy ears and busy, connected eyebrows. He led the way to a dreary examining room and sat himself down before offering Fran a chair. Two Great Danes watched from the hall.

"I hope Lys and Skygge didn't startle you. My patients use the front door."

At the sound of their names the dogs crowded the room, slavering and snorting and yawning, their whip-tailed rumps trembling in paroxysms of obeisance. Their master picked up the newspaper and shooed them away. Fran noticed it was that morning's *Republic*.

He asked about the Comstock case.

"Ruptured aneurysm. The pericardium was full of blood."

"Was there an autopsy?"

"I did what there was to do. The medical examiner countersigned the death certificate."

"Isn't the autopsy supposed to be done by a pathologist in cases involving unattended death?"

Dr. Tagen reconsidered Fran. "Sam's death came as no surprise. Chronic alcohol abuse takes its toll. I warned him often enough, but he had other priorities."

"Other priorities?"

"The burdens each of us carries through life and the ways we have of lightening the load."

"Did you run a blood-alcohol test?"

"Hardly needed to. When I opened him up he was just full of liquor."

Fran asked about the extent of mutilation.

"Pretty bad."

"Did it happen before or after death?"

"After."

"How did you determine that?"

"The damage was what you'd expect from postmortem wounds. The soft tissues of the face were stripped. The extremities received great attention. One of the arms was worried from the socket. A femur was crushed."

"What kind of animal would be capable of that?"

"A large dog would have the strength."

"Like a Great Dane?"

Dr. Tagen smiled his strange smile. "The Great Dane is a coward when it comes to the cold. I have to beat my two with your fine paper to get them outdoors to do their duty."

"How about a wild animal?"

"The flesh torn from the corpse wasn't eaten. It was scattered around. I might say playfully."

"So whatever did it wasn't very hungry."

"That was the conclusion we came to."

"We?"

"Malory Boulding and I."

"The chief of police."

On the way to the door Fran noticed a ponderous old writing table with cruel taloned legs sticking out from under the skirts. The books on top were at least as old, some leather-bound and others in loose bundles of parchment. They looked too old even to have been Dr. Tagen's medical school texts, and Fran asked him if he were interested in the history of medicine. Steel Harbor, the doctor said. The town went way back, an important port of call when Riverston was still a sawmill and a public house.

"It's all turned around now," Fran said.

"Town's like me." The old man scratched behind the ears of the big salt-and-pepper-spotted dog called Lys. "Dead and don't know it."

Back on the street Fran stopped to catch his breath, as if he had been holding it the whole time he was inside the doctor's house. The past was alive and breathing in that house, stealing air from the present.

He intended to make the inn his next stop, but, as he walked past the Town Building across the street, a police car followed by a pickup truck bristling with riflemen drove up the hill from the harbor and stopped in front. The men climbed out and stamped their feet and took off gloves and shooting mittens and blew on their hands, breath steaming. They wore civilian clothes and carried hunting rifles, except for the two policemen. One of the policemen cradled a pump shotgun in the crook of his arm. The other, who was not carrying a long gun, went inside while the rest stayed on the street lighting pipes and cigarettes and horsing around. Fran went over and introduced himself to the policeman with the shotgun. The men gathered round and showed off their guns when they heard Fran was a reporter.

"Didn't see a footprint," the policeman said. "Crust on the flats's so frigging hard that truck wouldn't leave tracks."

"They're running at night," a man said. "We won't catch nothing out there before dark."

"You won't catch me out there after," said another.

Yankee laughter. Crackly and parsimonious, like it cost something to laugh.

"Who you boys talking to out in the cold?" The policeman who had gone inside filled the doorway.

"Reporter from Riverston, Mal."

"Get your tails indoor before you freeze them off. You, too, reporter-from-Riverston."

Fran trooped in with the others, filling the foyer with cold, noise, smoke, the smell of gun oil and spruce gum. The town clerk, an extremely thin woman with extremely thin hair, buttoned up her cardigan and gave them all the evil eye.

"Chief Boulding?" Fran said to the policeman. The man had a fleshy face and fleshy lips, the upper partially concealed by a mustache grown perhaps for that purpose.

"That's right. Coffee . . . um?"

"Fran. Fran Thomas."

"Coffee, Fran?"

"I'm doing a story on the Comstock death for the *Republic,* and I'd like to hear about your search this morning."

"We are fresh out. Hazel, we are fresh out of the powdered creamer again."

"It's you men that drink all the coffee," the town clerk said. "I just can't be bothered."

"Any chance Comstock might have been attacked before he was dead?"

The chief handed Fran a styrofoam cup of oily black coffee, and turned to the men. "I'm going to talk to Fran in the office. Warm up and have some coffee." A disappointed look at Hazel. "Hope everybody likes it black."

He closed the door behind them and pointed to a chair. He took off his parka, revealing a muscular, heavyset body a lot fitter than his jowly face suggested. He was about Fran's age but looked older, like some NCOs — twenty-five going on fifty — Fran had known in the army.

"I'm going to help you all I can," the chief said. "But I need your help, too. The public needs to be educated with respect to the fact that the family pet in the unsupervised company of others like itself is a destructive element. Wildlife, livestock, even minors are in danger when dogs run in packs. Only last week they brought down a pretty little doe, ripped her guts out, didn't eat a bite, killed her for sport." He compressed those big lips and shook his head. "Make the public aware of the facts, Fran, and I'll owe you one."

There were two kinds of cops when it came to the press, those who avoided it and those who exploited it, and no matter how noble the motive, the second was the bigger nuisance. Fran repeated the question about Comstock having been attacked before he died.

"He might have been. He might have fallen down dead drunk. Alive but incapacitated. It all amounts to the same thing."

Fran pressed. He kept hearing about Comstock's alcoholism. But was there any real proof he was drunk that night? Why hadn't a simple test been done?

"This isn't New York," the chief said. "I know my town. Sam was under the influence, all right. His bottle is the only thing we found out there in two day's hunting."

"Somebody else could have dropped it."

"Who?"

Fran shrugged. "Woody Parker."

"Not likely."

"What about his story, then?"

"You mean wolves?" The chief tapped his forehead. "This is the whereabouts of Woody's wolves."

"He was first on the scene, wasn't he?"

The chief looked disappointed. "I thought I could count on you, Fran."

"You can count on me to do my job, and since all you have is a corpse and a vodka bottle, my job is to ask questions."

"That's my job, too, Fran." The chief opened his desk drawer and took out a clear plastic bag, the kind you get at the grocery store. In it was the broken glass neck and green label off a pint of Wolfschmidt vodka. "How did you know what kind of bottle it was?"

Fran might have said Dr. Tagen must have mentioned it until

he saw that green label. He shrank back into his skull and looked out at it through the eye holes. The chief was waiting.

"Would you believe me if I told you I think I dreamed it?"

The chief looked at him with glittery cop eyes.

5

THERE really was a widow's walk at the Widow's Walk Inn, and as Edna Sergeant had told Fran, there was a widow, too. The steep rooftop balcony looked nautical and treacherous, like its shipboard cousin, the widow maker. A section of railing was missing. Perhaps the deceased Mr. Parker had met his end in a fall. If a dream could come true, why not a name?

Fran entered a lobby with hardwood floors, Turkish rugs, and a spiral staircase with white balusters and a black handrail. The doorway to the left led to a coffee shop. He could see bright fixtures and smell hot coffee. He had been plied with so much of it that morning the smell turned his stomach. The doorway to the right was too dim to see much, but the smell was of a tavern before hours, yeasty and waxy and bitter with stale cigarette smoke. He went into the coffee shop where a man sat by himself at the counter, forking down a plate of bacon and eggs, and two elderly ladies whispered over pots of tea. The woman behind the counter listened in with a look of skeptical amusement drawn on her handsome face. Her expression didn't change when she considered Fran, as if he, too, were a morsel of gossip.

He told her who he was looking for and why. The solitary bacon-and-egg eater stopped eating. The whispering of the ladies ceased.

"Caroline's in the bar," the woman said. "Don't waste her time. She can do that for herself."

"You must be Mrs. Parker," Fran said. As he walked out, the eating and whispering picked up where they left off.

The taproom was stocked with wares from the glory days of the China trade. Fancy oriental iron work screened a fireplace faced with Dutch tiles, a Japanese landscape on rice paper hung next to an oil painting of a clipper ship, a hutch displayed pieces of pewter, scrimshaw, English and Cathay china. Chairs were stacked upside down on the tables, stools on the bar. The young woman sitting at a window seat beneath louvered blinds had the room to herself. She wore a long skirt that was bright like a quilt. Her copper-colored hair was pulled back, its frizzy ends giving off sparks in the sunlight that streaked through the blinds. She was bent over the ledger in her lap, one hand holding a pencil above the page, the other twirling a wisp of hair that had loosened down her ear. Her skin was redhead pale, but unfreckled, and she was homely in the beautiful way redheads sometimes are. Looking on the scene Fran felt he had stepped into the past a hundred years and was catching a glimpse of a private moment in the life of a woman whose secret joys and sorrows were lost to time like a ring lost in the ocean.

She looked up at him. In the first instant her eyes grew big and wild, like a shied horse, then they calmed and deepened. They were green as the sea with shallows of gray and depths of blue and made her otherwise plain face so pretty its sweetness was a pain to him.

"Caroline?"

Dry lips were moistened. She was not wearing makeup. In L.A. it would have been called the natural look, in Steel Harbor it was simply natural.

He said he was a reporter and wanted to talk to her uncle about Sam Comstock's death. She was suspicious.

"I don't want to expose Uncle Woody to ridicule." Her voice was strained, like there was a lot back there that wasn't getting out.

"I'll write what he tells me. Straight."

She closed the ledger and stood up. She was tall, with childlike buds of breasts and hips in full womanly bloom, in her late twenties, although the innocent skin made her age hard to guess.

"Without your uncle all I have is an interesting obit."

She was making up her mind about him. He could tell by the way she stalled for time. She put the ledger away behind the bar and began breaking rolls of coins into the cash register.

"It might be good if somebody besides me listened to him," she said.

"My job is to listen."

"Don't."

"What?"

"Patronize me."

He flushed.

She smiled to herself. "Give me a chance to change."

He waited in the taproom. He heard her cross the lobby and go into the coffee shop. He heard her talking to her mother. He couldn't hear what they were saying but he heard the way they said it. Mrs. Parker was sarcastic and Caroline was humorless. No, humoring. The daughter humored the mother and that only encouraged the woman.

When Caroline came back she was wearing a powder blue parka and white jeans. He had first seen her in the long skirt, and now the white denim against her long thighs made her seem shockingly naked below the waist. She looked down at herself.

"Is something wrong?"

"Sorry. It's just that you're very pretty."

She let out a grunt of discomfort.

They took the VW north at the crossroads. A short ways out of town they pulled over into a turnout cleared by the plow. They got out of the car and followed the trail down into the woods. Caroline led the way. She took long strides, and even though she lugged a canvas tote full of goodies for her uncle, the pace she set was all Fran could handle. He coveted her insulated gum boots.

"City slicker, huh?" she said, glancing back. She had some of the Down East accent, enough to drop her r's and flatten her vowels — city slicka.

"I was born in Maine," he said. "Before this fall I spent the last ten years in California."

"Why'd you come back?"

"I missed being miserable."

They came out of the woods into a meadow rolling with snow-drifts. He heard water gurgling hollowly somewhere below. Soon they were directly over it.

"I've never seen Whiskey Springs freeze up," she said.

"The new ice age." Out here in the middle of a glacial meadow, standing on frozen-over running water, the chatter of the TV weathermen became grimly credible.

"Uncle Woody says the narrows have frozen up, too, and that's salt water."

"Is that where he found the body?"

The pompon on the back of her cap bounced affirmatively.

"Far from here?"

The pompon wagged the negative.

On the far side of the meadow he saw the opening through the trees where the path continued down to the mud flats. He couldn't see them but he smelled them — briny, rotten. He smelled wood smoke, too. A cabin and outbuildings were set back against the north border of the meadow. He had expected a tarpaper shack, but the place was built like a blockhouse, of fieldstone with high shuttered windows. The door was rough oak. It opened as they came up.

"S-s-seen you coming," the voice inside said with a stutter sibilant like the hiss of a tea kettle.

Caroline stepped in and hugged a hulking old fellow in a flannel shirt and suspenders that held up a pair of coarse wool pants. He gave Fran a withering handshake and spat a cud of tobacco into the snow before shutting the door. A kitchen wood stove dominated the center of the cabin like a pagan altar. There was just the one big room, with raw stone walls and a plank floor covered by scraps of linoleum. The iron smell of water from the sink pump and the cistern of the stove took Fran back to his grandparents' farmhouse.

Caroline unpacked her tote bag. There were eggs, a quart of milk rattling with ice, homemade bread, mince pie. Woody was all for warming up the pie and dividing it then and there, but Caroline said it was for him and she wouldn't eat a bite.

"Me and this young fella will do it justice then, won't we, Bub?" he said, giving Fran a cuff. He put the pie into the oven, added wood and shook out the ash, all the while clicking his tongue against his palate. He reminded Fran of a trained bear.

For all the spry bluster there was something brittle about Woody, a nerve stretched thin as a scream. The big bear-paw hands trembled, and the tobacco-stained corners of his mouth worked as if he heard unsettling voices. Fran took in the rugged door, its peephole and bolt, the fortress-thick walls, the traps and ropes hanging above the workbench at the back of the cabin.

"Care to see the shop?" Woody was taking in Fran, too.

In the warm months he made his living as a mason. He showed Fran his squares and trowels, his levels lovingly wrapped in rags, his blocks and tackle. Fran was more interested in the clump of steel traps and chains hanging from rings set in the mortar.

"Those used to be my winter work. Earnt a little extra trapping varmints."

"What kind?"

"Mus-s-s-krat, otter, fox. Rabbit for the stewpot."

"How about the big one?" The rusty trap Fran pointed out was three times the size of the others. The clamped jaws had peg teeth with gaps between, as if in old age the trap had lost all but the ten or so left in its tight, grim smile.

"Never had call to use that one. A curiosity, you might say. That's an old Newhouse wolf trap."

It was time he identified himself.

When Woody heard that Fran was a reporter he turned on his niece. "You knew about this gink."

"I thought talking about it might help, Uncle Woody."

"Talking about it," he minced with heavy irony. "Those are woman's ways, not mine. If you can't abide by my ways maybe you better not come down no more."

Fran was still wondering why Woody never had use for a wolf trap if, as he claimed, wolves killed Sam Comstock. He asked him.

"Nobody catches these wolves," Woody said with the craftiness of a crazy man. "They do the catching."

Maybe the chief was right about him, after all.

"Have you seen them?" Fran asked outright.

"Not lately."

"When?"

"Long ago."

"Where?"

"The neck."

"Where's that?"

Woody took it into his head not to answer. He clicked.

"Wolf Neck," Caroline said. "Wolf Neck is the old-time name for the islands. Isn't that right, Uncle Woody?"

"My pie!" Woody hopped to the stove and opened the oven door. The smell of scorched currants and molasses and venison suet carried on the blast of dry heat.

Fran remembered his grandfather using the name Wolf Neck. There could have been wolves on the islands. Once.

"If you didn't see them, what makes you so sure they did the killing?"

Woody stabbed the blackened crust with his jackknife and let out a cloud of spicy steam.

Fran tried another approach. "When was the last time you saw Sam alive?"

Woody licked the sticky blade.

"Didn't he have to pass by here that night?"

"There's another way," Caroline said. "Through the quarry from town. I walk there sometimes."

" 'Course he went that way," Woody grumbled. "I heard his s-s-singing."

Caroline and Fran looked at each other.

"You didn't mention this before, Uncle Woody."

"Nobody asked before."

"How could you hear that distance?" What Fran really wanted to know was what song Sam had been singing. He had no idea why.

Woody went to his cot and sat down. "Sometimes at night when it's clear and there ain't a wind I can stand in the dooryard and hear them howl. You have to know how to listen. You slow your heart and listen between beats." The sweat poured off him. "That's how I heard that pitiful outlaw s-s-singing in the flats. I knew right where to look next morning."

"Why didn't you stop him?"

"Go out there at night?" Woody put his hands over his ears. "You don't know what you're asking."

What song? The urge to ask made Fran squirm like the urge to laugh in church. But Woody was beyond answering any more questions. He balled up on the cot with his face to the wall. Caroline made signs for Fran to leave.

"Thanks for your help, Mr. Parker. Sorry about the pie."

Caroline opened the door. She was staying behind. He saw that she had already put him out of her mind. In the winter light slicing through the open doorway her eyes had the blue translucence of glacier ice.

"He gone yet?" came a petulant voice from the cot.

Fran made his way along the path toward the road. He stopped at the hidden brook and looked back across the meadow at the cabin against the dark spruce. The third little pig had built his house of brick rather than stone. But for the same purpose.

6

HE was playing in his favorite childhood place. Over the hill from the farm was a woodlot that had been an even older farm that had also belonged to the Thomas family. And through the lot ran a lane that went down to the tidelands, passing cellar holes and stone walls and the little graveyard full of old-time Thomases.

It was Christmas. He knew because of the snow. He and his mother and father came for a week every summer and a week every Christmas. There had been an ice storm, too. The birches and young larches were bent with ice and jangled like chimes in the salt breeze, and the crust on the snow was just thick enough to fool him into trusting it.

He stood at the graveyard gate, looking in. A stone wall surrounded it square. It was not much bigger than one of the old foundations. Oak trees grew among the slate tombstones. No Thomas had been buried here since the Civil War. One of the stones had a brass plaque marking the resting place of Major Francis Thomas, hero of the Canadian campaign of the War of 1812 and delegate to the first Maine Constitutional Convention. He was the only famous person the family had produced, and, according to Grampy Thomas, would ever produce — if their luck didn't run out. The boy's vision of the old major was a cross between the picture of George Washington on a dollar bill and the oak tree with the rotten limb that crowded the gravestone.

On the snow between the granite gateposts at the entrance to the graveyard he saw the footprints of an animal heavy enough to leave tracks without breaking through the crust. They came out but didn't go in. He followed them down the lane towards the cove. They padded along through the ice tunnel made by the overhanging trees. He came out of the twinkly shade into the glare of open water, his view of the bay cut off by the reach of cliff topped with pine trees that looked like an Indian face with a

Mohawk haircut. His grandfather said that Steel Harbor and a place the old-timers called Wolf Neck lay beyond. The boy wondered how any timer could be older than Grampy Thomas.

The tracks ended at the tidehead where the ice was scrolled over the sea straw. In the clickety-click of branches behind he heard laughter. He turned and saw a woman, pale as the moon, in a thin white gown standing among the trees. She gave him a look no woman gives a boy, and it was as a man that he looked back and as a man that he followed when she turned into the woods.

She padded barefoot up the hill and he could not catch her because he kept breaking through the crust. As she passed over the top, he saw her set off against the winter sky. Her gown was made of snowflakes and he could see her nakedness beneath. She gave him a bold look, and he saw her eyes for the first time. They were not human.

Before he had time to be afraid she was on her way down the other side. The white clapboard house and the barn that had once been white came into view through the trees. He followed her across the yard and into the house. The doors and windows were open and snow blew across the floor and icicles hung in the stairwell. They went upstairs and down a hall. She opened the door at the end and warm sunlight burst through. She turned to him and smiled. It was a smile of incredible sweetness, so sunny, so strangely familiar, that he felt he had always known her even though he had never seen her before. The room to her back was full of spring flowers and a tree — a fragrant tree growing right in the room — a living garden, an outside inside. The snowflake gown melted and left her brassy wet.

| | | |

This dream he remembered. The nostalgia it left him with was overwhelming. But who was she? He felt a longing as real as if she herself had been real. He went through the morning half in a trance, pretending to be awake, and from time to time he remembered that he could not remember her and felt a rush of sweetness that was like the touch of music on the skin.

Susan? He still dreamed of his ex-wife, but she was always a solid presence up to specific mischief. Besides, Susan was an edgy brunette with a taut, gymnast's body, not at all like the snow queen of his dream. Caroline Parker? There was more of a physical likeness, but why couldn't he remember the face? He had just spent the previous morning with her. How about a premonition — a woman he hadn't met yet? He smiled at that.

In the afternoon he came back from an assignment and found two memos on his desk. One was neat as typescript, the other barely legible. The first said that a Professor Swanson from the university had called to speak to the reporter "responsible" for the story about the Steel Harbor wolves. The second said, "See me."

Fran glanced across the newsroom through the cubicle window into Ray's empty office. He asked Tommy Blackburn at the desk nearest his if he'd seen Ray. Tommy was running his daily race with deadline, hurried fingers stumbling across the typewriter. He was a skier, and had a skier's winter sunburn and a skier's habit of watching the clock Friday afternoon.

"He's been looking for you," Tommy said, eye on the clock.

"What for?"

"Love to chat, Fran, but some of us have work to do."

Ray wasn't in layout or hanging around the copy desk, but one of the women said she had seen him in the morgue with Angela. That was good for a few laughs. Angela DeGregorio was an ambitious young copy clerk, pretty and flirtatious and an object of suspicion among some of her co-workers. The first memo on Fran's desk had been in her scrupulous hand.

He went downstairs to the file library on the ground floor near the presses and walked in on Ray chewing Angela out.

"You've rigged things down here so only you can find anything," Ray said. "There are more productive ways of making yourself indispensable." Angela's eyes brimmed with tears that hadn't quite begun to spill over.

"What do you want?" he said when he saw Fran.

"To save beauty from the beast."

Angela's grateful smile squeezed out a few tears.

"Cheap shot," Ray said.

Angela had some exotic kind of bone cancer. The disease was in remission, but a series of operations had crippled one leg and chemotherapy had streaked her raven hair silver even though she was still in her early twenties. She walked with a cane or crutches, depending on how she felt that day. Some days she didn't come in at all. Ray looked after her. He had seen to it that she receive more than her share of insurance benefits and salary for time off. He had three daughters at home and treated Angela as the fourth, a relationship some upstairs in the newsroom chose to interpret as incestuous.

"Congratulations on making the wire service," she said to Fran to maneuver Ray onto another subject.

"Oh, yeah," Ray said. "The wire picked up your Steel Harbor piece. We'll budget a follow-up for Monday. Talk to the professor. Do some digging."

Fran felt a deep excitement to be back on the story. He had thought it was dead. Digging into it was somehow like digging into his own past. He asked about his other assignment and Ray told him to hold over the weekend and if he got behind to use Angela. Her eager black eyes made him an offer that seemed to extend beyond a professional joining of forces. Word had gotten around the newsroom that he was a burnout case from the majors. Ray's two cripples.

Back at his desk he dialed the number Professor Swanson had left and found himself connected to the biology department at the university. The secretary put him through and a woman answered. Yes, she was Professor Swanson.

Fran said he was the reporter "responsible" for the story in the morning *Republic.*

"A colleague brought the article to my attention," she said. "I did field work in wolf pack communications last year at Coronation Island." There was a likable chattiness in her voice despite the jargon.

"That's not here in Maine?"

"Southern Alaska, and there lies the problem. There hasn't been a documented sighting of a wolf in Maine this century. That's why I can't understand why the man you quoted was so adamant. And frankly, it disturbs me that you would print his statement without documentation."

"I'm a reporter, not a scientist, Professor Swanson."

"Be that as it may, until recently wolves have received a rather bad press." She was earnest but not strident, a woman who prided herself on her reasonableness. He tried to imagine her, this reasonable lady biologist, tape recorder strapped to her shoulder, running with the pack.

"I tried to give the reader the impression that the wolf theory was just one man's opinion."

"Where wolves are concerned, it takes very little to set off a witch hunt. Your article may be reprinted in states where there are still struggling wolf populations and lend itself to further oppression."

"The wire service did pick it up."

"There you are."

Fran had a motive for being so reasonable himself. He told her he was doing a follow-up and wanted to talk to her in depth. "You know," he said, "some scientific trivia about wolves spiced with a little bleeding-heart environmentalist oratory." Somehow he knew that she would not take offense at this, that this was precisely the way to approach her.

"In that case I have a proposition for you," she said. "Do you ski?"

Fran glanced over at Tommy Blackburn drowning his sorrows in a can of Mountain Dew. "I used to."

"I'm going down to see for myself in the morning and I've been told that the Channel Islands are accessible only by crossing the frozen marshes. I'm bringing my cross-country skis. Care to come along?"

They agreed to meet at the coffee shop at the inn. She asked if he would introduce her to Woody Parker. He said they hadn't exactly hit it off but he could introduce her to Woody's niece.

"I'm looking forward to working with you, Mr. Thomas."

"Fran."

"Good-bye then, Fran."

"Good-bye, Professor Swanson."

"Wilma."

Swanson, he thought after hanging up. Scandinavian. Probably a true blond. A big girl. Athletic and trim. Skin as cool as a mountain freshet. He imagined them spending a vigorous day outdoors together, she in search of wolves, he of a story. And later, indoors, warmed by a crackling fire — he imagined more.

"Tommy, I need some advice."

"Later, Fran."

"I need some advice about skis."

Tommy looked at the clock. "Guess I'm gonna be here a while anyway."

"I need a pair of cross-country skis."

Tommy turned up his nose as if his delicate sensibilities had been offended. "I thought you meant real skiing."

Fran said he was going out early in the morning and needed to rent them that night. A suggestion of skullduggery crossed Tommy's bland, handsome face. A buddy of his worked at a local sporting goods store. He could give him a call and fix Fran up before they closed.

"Hey, thanks, Tommy."

"No sweat. Say, Fran, you're the new hotshot on the block.

I 41 I

How about taking a look at this?" He handed over his copy and notes. "Maybe you could suggest a couple of things."

Soon Fran was revising Tommy's story while Tommy gabbed over the phone about the upcoming weekend at Sugarloaf with his buddy at the sporting goods store. Suddenly Fran stopped work, looked up, and stared right through Tommy.

"The dream woman," he said. "Maybe she really was a premonition."

7

FRAN pulled up behind the Land Cruiser parked outside the Widow's Walk Inn. The vertical rack on the rear of the vehicle held a pair of cross-country skis. He was early, a habit of his, but Wilma Swanson was earlier.

On the way up the walk he stopped and looked at the thermometer outside the coffee shop window. Zero degrees Fahrenheit — not bad compared to some mornings this cold snap. He stepped closer and looked in the window. He saw a woman in an Icelandic sweater, skiing knickers, and red sports gaiters sitting at the counter with her back to him. It was a very promising back, tapered at the shoulders and slim in the waist with a single braid of straw-colored hair lying down the spine. Suddenly he was looking into another face as close to the inside of the window as his was to the outside. The large sea-green eyes were startled; then the lids narrowed at the outer corners and the pale lips flattened to suggest a smile. Caroline Parker motioned for him to step back so she could read the thermometer.

The woman at the counter turned and faced him as he came in. She had broad cheekbones pitted with acne scars and the thoughtful eyes that so often seem to accompany the condition.

"Wilma?"

"You must be Fran."

She was not the Norse goddess of his fantasy, and closer to forty than he was, but she glowed with calmness and vitality, and he felt the magnetism of a nurturing heart when they nudged shoulders as he took the stool next to hers. The reasonableness he had been conscious of over the phone was really a kind of sympathetic intelligence. She was not wearing a wedding ring, and he guessed right away that wolves were her babies.

"I saw your rig outside," he said.

"My one self-indulgence," she said in her analytical way. "A colleague claims it's my way of letting my hair down."

Mrs. Parker, in scarlet lipstick and smoking a cigarette, took their order. Caroline remained by the window with her arms folded, watching the sun struggle up. Fran introduced her to Wilma. He said Wilma was a scientist and wanted to talk to her uncle.

"I won't press him," Wilma said.

"Just your being there will press him." Caroline looked at Fran. "Can't you understand that?"

"Offer him a free lunch and he'll talk," Mrs. Parker said as she poured the coffee. "I've lost track of all the grub he's freeloaded around here."

"Mother."

Fran could almost hear teeth grinding as Caroline suppressed a shout of rage.

By now everybody felt uncomfortable enough for Mrs. Parker to be satisfied with a job well done, so she stuffed out her lipstick-stained cigarette in the ashtray near Fran and moved down the counter to wait on Hazel, the town clerk, who had just come in. Hazel thought that Mrs. Parker was a card.

After breakfast Fran secured his skis next to Wilma's on the back of the Land Cruiser. She said they had one stop to make in town before they left. The police chief.

Fran made a face.

"He could be right about feral dogs, you know. They often turn out to be responsible for predation blamed on wolves. I'd like to examine the doe he told you about."

"He won't help you."

"He was very helpful over the phone. He said I could see her."

Mal Boulding was waiting in his office. His hair was freshly cut and smelled of Lilac Vegetal, the part white as a scar. He treated Wilma like a fellow public servant because of her connection with the university. "I saved the carcass in case somebody from the state wanted a look."

When he saw Fran he made a face a lot like the one Fran had made. "He with you?" he said to Wilma.

They followed the chief out to his place on the Whiskey Springs road. Wilma drove like a maniac. She speeded up on turns for the thrill of down shifting out of four-wheel-drive skids. The boxy cab of the Land Cruiser tipped this way and that.

The police car turned into the driveway of a farmhouse with a swayback barn. Wilma stopped and took out a small leather case and a 35-millimeter camera. The chief held the barn door for them. Inside, the cold seemed colder because it was so still. There was an ammoniac smell of hay and manure, and the sunlight leaking through the roof and walls cast a grid of bright and gloom. The doe hung above their heads from the main beam by a rope noosed at the crossed rear shanks. The hyperextended torso stretched down from graceful thighs along the tapered belly to the swell of the brisket. Black blood caked the rubbery nose. Glassy eyes stared amazed at the prospect of eternity.

Wilma reached up and separated the icy folds of the lips and inspected the teeth. "Five years old," she said.

The chief was impressed. Here was an expert from the state university who knew a thing or two. He let down the rope until the forelegs brushed the floor.

"Look at these wounds," she said to Fran.

What came into the light was gaping, appalling. Ragged flesh had been left hanging. There was even a sort of *coup de grâce* wound to the back of the neck, as if once the doe had been brought down but still thrashing, she was hit from behind to avoid and paralyze the punishing hooves. Wilma examined the neck wound first. She took a pair of surgical scissors and a scalpel from the case and cut away the frozen gore and snipped the tendon to the bone.

"Cervical vertebrae crushed."

"Must have been what finished her," the chief agreed.

"I'd like to examine the heart."

The chief nodded as if he expected as much, expected such attention to detail, such thoroughness, from a representative of the state university.

Wilma swung the carcass around and exposed the white underbelly and flag. She made an incision and stripped away a flap of hide below the rib cage and cut in under the diaphragm. The frosty membranous tissue peeled back with the sound of sandpaper on soft wood. The slippery tallow thawed against the warmth of her hands and the chief had to hold the body cavity open for her. Fran saw the blood-filled pericardial sac as Wilma exposed the heart. It looked like a ruptured hot-water bottle filled with dark pudding.

"Her heart burst," Wilma said. "That was the cause of death. What I can't understand is why so little was eaten."

"Dogs," said the chief, releasing his hold and slipping in half thawed suet and blood as he stepped back.

Wilma wasn't so sure. She looked again at the crushed vertebrae. She attached the flash to her camera and took pictures. After a thoughtful pause: "Sometimes wolves will leave a kill intending to come back and before they do the prey is found by man."

The chief was disappointed that Wilma would even consider the wolf theory. He turned his scowl on Fran as if he were the culprit. Disappointment became alarm.

"Are you all right?"

Fran's heart pounded. He had seen the flash of the camera pulse in the deer's dead eye. He saw the gore shiny on Wilma's hands, the tuft of bloody hair in the lacing of the chief's boot, the breath steaming from their nostrils, and the absence of breath from that rubbery black nose. He smelled lilac after-shave mixed with the sweet stench of the slaughterhouse and the cold sourness of the barn. And in the silence following the shutter click and ratchety rewind of the camera he heard a creaking that he thought was the sigh of settling timbers — until he saw the slow twisting of the doe. She was a pendulum swaying on her rope that high in the rafters chaffed the crossbeam. The barn had become a giant clock.

At that moment Wilma looked at him, her pocked forehead anointed with a dark dab of blood.

"I said are you all right?"

He turned into the shadows and was sick.

The chief took him outside. He wiped his face with fresh snow and ate some to get the taste of vomit out of his mouth. He felt better. Wilma came out a minute later. The spot of blood was gone. Had it ever been there?

"What happened in there?" she said.

"I don't know. It was like I was dreaming awake."

8

THEY parked in the turnout to Woody's meadow and prepared their skis. Fran waxed quickly and haphazardly and was soon on the trail. Soon, too, he was remembering things — how to use the poles for speed and balance, how to turn without heel support, and how, as soon as you were moving on skis, the cold couldn't touch you. He stopped at the woods and waited for Wilma. Methodical and thorough, she finished waxing and laid out her skis. She stepped into them and secured the toe bindings and taking up her poles and stepping off like a skater she glided down beside him. Her lips were glossy with sun block.

They set off through the pine trees. The distance that two days before had taken half an hour to walk they covered in minutes. At the hidden brook he pointed out the cabin across the meadow. Smoke was coming from the chimney. They skied up to the door and Fran released his bindings and knocked. The padlock was attached to the staple with the hasp free. He knocked again.

"It's Fran Thomas, Mr. Parker. I talked to Caroline a while ago."

No answer. He walked around back to the privy and woodshed with cordwood spilling out the door. A maul ax was wedged into the chopping block. A pair of snowshoes hung against the wall.

"Mr. Parker?" he called.

A raven answered from the woods, then silence.

"I thought sure he'd be home when I saw smoke," Wilma said, coming around with his skis.

He put a finger to his lips and hushed her. They pushed off. Away from the cabin he said, "I think he is home. I think he's been watching us all along." They glanced back, then quickly looked away.

"Is he emotionally disturbed?"

"Scared."

"Of us?"

"Of whatever it is that's down there." He nodded toward the path that dipped into the tideland woods.

They found the going easy. A set of snowshoe tracks had broken trail and packed the snow with repeated use. Fran wondered what compelled the hermit to return again and again to the place he dreaded. It was like a child checking the closet for the boogeyman before turning out the light.

The trail was a long slide down. Pine gave way to swamp hardwoods and these in turn lost out to sumac and cattails as the curtain of woods was drawn back on a sunken prairie rimmed by a horizon of choppy winter sea. The nearest island, bristling with spruce like a sleeping porcupine, lay in the distance across the snowfield.

Wilma poked the icy crust with her ski pole. "We won't find any tracks on this."

Fran asked how she could tell wolf tracks from dog even if they found some. Wilma splayed her fingers inside her mitten and showed him how a wolf's paw was built like a snowshoe. She poked two sets of marks in the crust. The narrowness of a wolf's thorax allowed the rear legs to follow in line with the front whereas the rear legs of a dog followed between. The scats were another clue.

"You mean wolf shit?"

"A great deal can be ascertained from the scats."

"And I thought a reporter had a tough life."

They set out for the islands with Wilma in the lead. The great open space turned each of them inward and they did not speak all the way across. The big muscles in Fran's legs burned. His face burned in the glare of sunshine off the dazzling ice. Icicles of snot froze to his upper lip. The rhythmic slide of Wilma's body was hypnotic, and he found himself concentrating on her metronomic buttocks pumping beneath the wool knickers. It made him think of the carrion clock in the barn.

She pulled up short and he ran up her skis. They had come flush to the open channel. He looked into the winter-clear water and saw smooth stones deep down and wavering kelp abutted by shelves of ice. The bridge across had been formed by ice pans dislodged upstream on the flood tide and carried seaward on the ebb to where the flotage had jammed the neck. The passage was narrow, fissured, and slick. Wilma went first.

On the other side they found pink blood stains that had seeped into the crust. Bits of cloth adhered to the ice. Human hair. The snow along the woodline was tramped with bootprints. Fran picked up a spent shotgun shell.

Deeper in the woods they came to undisturbed powder and Wilma took heart. A sea breeze blew through the high spruce boughs. The forest floor was shaded and sharp with the smell of cold pine and the sun shone through in patches. They came to a clearing on a sheltered cove where a young whitetail buck was licking sea salt among the frozen reeds. They were downwind so he hadn't caught their scent, and the cattail stalks crackled under his hooves so he hadn't heard them. Wilma froze when she saw him, but Fran crouched to make himself less conspicuous. The narrow face and spreading rack pointed in his direction, the goggle eyes locking on the point where they had sensed movement. For ten long seconds they stared at one another, and just when it seemed to Fran the buck would never move, he bolted, veering hard right, hooves smashing cattails and clattering on the ice, skipping into deep snow, past them, downwind and into the woods where he melted away so perfectly that just a single low-lying pine bough lost its burden of snow. Plash.

Fran wondered how even a wolf could catch an animal so nimble. Wilma said it was a matter of economy of energy. Wolves preferred to harvest the young and infirm.

"Does more than bucks?"

"That's a myth."

Fran despised the misuse of that powerful word to mean generally held misconception.

"Our culture likes to believe that wolves select does," Wilma went on. "The predatory male possessing the passive female."

"Male chauvinist wolves?"

"It goes against the stereotype to think of a bitch wolf pulling down a buck. That's why objective studies are so important. To understand wolves we must first demythologize them."

"And demythologizing the wolf is sort of your holy mission in life." He looked to see if he had gotten a rise out of her, but he had not. Even scientists had their blind spots.

To gain the head of the second island they had to cross an icy spit. The second was larger than the first and seemed to belong to a far more northern latitude. The conifers were stunted and windblown. The granite shore was beset by the crash and spray of huge incoming winter breakers. Slabs of fluted rock descended in a stairway to the sea where vast mussel beds colonized the shoals. Wilma left her skis and climbed down to a tidal pool while Fran remained on the ledge. She took off her mittens and dislodged a mussel with an instrument from her case, pried it open, and brought the dripping meat to her nose. Fran thought she was going to eat it. But she tossed the shell into the pool and came scrabbling back up the rocks.

"What was that all about?"

"I was wondering if wolves had a taste for shellfish."

She explained that wolves often had a backup food supply to see them through times of primary prey scarcity. Field mice on the tundra, Arctic hares on Ellesmere Island, harbor seals on Coronation Island, and maybe, the slimmest maybe, mussels on the Channel Islands.

"The kind of maybe that could make somebody's reputation," Fran said.

Talk of food made them hungry and they found a sheltered spot inland to have lunch. Wilma had brought along packets of trail food, serious-looking nourishment that wouldn't have been out of place on an Everest ascent. Fran took a mashed, half-frozen salami grinder from Jimmy's out of the cargo pocket of his flight jacket. He peeled off the cellophane and the smell of garlicky salad oil made his mouth ache. He was hungry as a . . .

"Wolves don't scare you at all?" he said right before taking a big bite.

"I respect them."

"Yeah, but if you were walking down a lonely road at night and heard howling behind you, wouldn't you walk a little faster?" he said with his mouth full.

"You're talking about a fear of the unknown, not wolves. I'm only human. As a child I read Paul de Kruif's *Microbe Hunters* and the part about Pasteur and the mad dogs gave me nightmares for weeks." She wiped a shred of coconut from her lower lip. "A colleague says my fear isn't of rabies but emotion."

This time when Fran climbed into his skis he felt no surge of warming energy. A shivery weariness crept over him like the desire for sleep. They retraced their trail to the spit where Wilma wanted to ski back by a new route. As they skirted a backwater of dirty ice and drowned trees, a raven high in the branches of a dead hemlock let out a squawk. Wilma went closer. The raven rocked from foot to foot and peered down at her with one brassy eye and then the other. Fran said the bird reminded him of Mrs. Parker.

"Ravens follow wolves," Wilma said. "Too bad it doesn't work the other way around."

The hemlock had been uprooted by frost and leaned at an angle. Something caught Wilma's attention and she squatted down on her skis and raked her pole in among the tangle of exposed roots. All Fran saw was frozen clay streaked with salt and rot. Out came a coral-colored object a foot long and half as wide, bulbous at one end and tapered at the other. She brushed off the silt and held it up.

"A wolf's, I think."

The skull was similar to those Fran had seen at the tar pits, this one less robust, and salt-bleached rather than darkly oiled. The lower jaw was missing, but most of the teeth of the upper were intact, sharp and the color of living bone. The smooth orbits of the eye sockets reflected the glow of the reddening sun.

"How can you tell it's not a dog's?" Somehow he knew it wasn't.

Wilma placed the flat of her hand along the side of the brow. She couldn't be positive until she made some measurements back at the lab, but the narrow orbital angle indicated Eastern Timber Wolf. The skull had been in the ground a long time. All it proved was that wolves had once inhabited the islands. Still. She gazed into it like a crystal ball. What good condition it was in. The frost must have dislodged it in pushing up the tree. She searched some more, gave a little cry of discovery, and reached in among the roots and snatched out a lean and wickedly serrated object the same coral color as the skull. The mandible. She couldn't believe it. They were usually broken into fragments. She fitted the hinged joint of the lower jaw to the upper, and the teeth made a sharp little clack as they interlocked. What luck.

A shriek startled them. The raven had landed on the snow nearby and strutted about with its head cocked to one side giving Wilma a greedy eye.

"He thinks we've found something to eat." She put the skull in her field pack. "Finders keepers, Buster."

The raven sassed back, shook its tail feathers, defecated, and took off. Its wings beat heavily on the darkening air.

They crossed the spit and made their way along the western shore of the landward island. Fran took the lead. The sun was dropping fast and he didn't want Wilma sidetracking them again. Halfway to the narrows they came to a rickety boathouse with a crooked tin chimney and a window wedged kitty-cornered under the peak of the roof. The boat ramp was stove up by stacking channel ice. Just beyond they found snowmobile tracks.

"These obscenities are destroying the winter habitat," Wilma said.

"The trail of this obscenity is going to get us out of here before dark." There was relief in Fran's voice.

"That's not the point."

Maybe not, but when he glanced back he saw that she, too, had taken to the packed trail. The caterpillar track led straight to the ice bridge and cut a runway across. They scooted over just as the treetops on the mainland were silhouetted in the setting sun. The snow shone pink as living skin.

Fran took a deep breath when he was off the islands, like the first breath after a high, deep dive. They skated across the flats toward the sinking light and away from the rising darkness. By degrees Fran became aware of a high-pitched whine. He looked back and saw a wolflike animal racing towards them out of an orb of white light. The animal's ears were flattened back for speed and the panting tongue lolled between its flying feet.

"Wilma, behind you!"

Fran swooshed to a stop and jumped out of his skis. He dug his heel into the crust and braced a pole at the ready with the aluminum tip aimed squarely at the charging animal's chest.

"It's a husky," Wilma said. "Put that down before you hurt him."

The animal made a complete circle around them, nails scraping the crust as he skidded sideways. He had a dense, silvery pelt and held his tail high without wagging it. He did not bark and his eyes were ghost blue.

"You sure that's a dog?"

"There's a little wolf in there somewhere," Wilma said. She squatted down and the husky rushed up and gave her a kiss.

A snowmobile bore down on them, gliding in with smooth, swooping speed. The headlamp hovered as if the machine moved through air instead of over snow. The noise was deafening after the day of snowy silence. The rider pulled alongside them and cut his engine.

"Saw your trail back there. Wondered if you made it out okay." His voice was surprisingly soft.

"We made it fine," Wilma said.

The zippered snowmobile suit and crash helmet added to the impression of flight. He flipped up the visor and revealed the face of a blue-eyed Tartar, the nose snub and the cheekbones high, the eyes slits of polished beryl.

"Ed Hentov."

"Fran Thomas. This is Professor Swanson."

"And that's Bullets."

He wore a lever-action rifle slung across one shoulder and nylon rope coiled over the other. He put his hand to the rope.

"How about a tow?"

"We managed this far by ourselves." Wilma's eyes were on the rifle. Fran noticed; Hentov did, too.

"Coyotes," he said. "That's my idea of what's been happening out here."

"You've been coyote hunting?" Wilma pronounced the *e* on the end; Hentov didn't.

"I'm a deer hunter. The deer come to the marsh licks in winter and the coyotes have come for the deer."

"You want to shoot coyotes now so there will be more deer for you to shoot in the fall, is that it?"

The man smiled, the kind of quiet smile that baffles a woman and is meant to. "Come on, Bullets." He lowered his visor and started the engine and with a parting nod gunned off across the flats with the husky close behind. The smell of oily gas hung on the twilight cold.

"I couldn't help it," Wilma said.

9

THE taproom at the Widow's Walk Inn entertained different clientele in winter and summer. In summer, well-to-do guests from out of state stayed in the upstairs bedrooms, and after day trips to Blue Hill and evening jaunts to Camden Playhouse, sipped their gin and tonics downstairs before retiring. Natives stayed away, driving instead to roadhouses along the shore route and downtown Riverston bars. But in winter, after the summer people left and the roads turned bad, the locals made the taproom their own, reasserting themselves like chickadees after the departure of the pushy but less hearty robins.

There was a good house tonight. And a good beech fire. Caroline Parker waited on tables and helped her bartender, Manly Howard, keep up. She was cheerful, efficient, and a little stupid — the way very private people are stupid in public. This suited the clientele, winter and summer. She didn't get the jokes the men told and that made the jokes better. She was quick to sympathize with the women without seeing through them. Serious. Sweet. Puzzled. Everybody loved Caroline and nobody knew her.

She was clearing off a table when the outside door opened and a draft rushed in and excited the fire. The air was as chilled as vodka left overnight in the freezer. She opened her mouth and caught some of the coolness on her tongue. A man and woman came in. They were dressed in heavy outdoor gear that radiated the cold, their faces chapped raw and their eyebrows and nostrils frosty. They stamped their feet and tugged at frozen zippers. The woman's scarf was stiff with ice at her mouth. Pearls of frost clung to the fleece cuffs and collar of the man's leather jacket, and when he took it off icicles fell and shattered on the floor.

"We made it," he said. His eyes were dilated with night. Caroline didn't want them looking at her, seeking her out.

"Did you find Uncle Woody?" she asked the woman.

"There was no answer when we knocked this morning. The cabin was dark tonight."

"He must have been out," Caroline said.

"Or wanted us to think so," the man put in.

She pretended not to hear. They sat at the table she had cleared and ordered mulled cider with brown rum. As she walked away she felt his eyes on her.

"Do you find her attractive?" she overheard the woman ask. She didn't hear his answer.

She saw to their drinks. She poured a skimpy shot of rum into one and a generous shot into the other and served the weak drink to the woman and strong one to the man. She did not know that she did this. He wrapped his hands around the warm mug and took a sip. His eyes watered, blinked, went to hers in thanks. His eyes were dark and deep, each a night to get lost in.

The woman was talking about an island in Alaska. Cut off from known wolf ranges. Close to civilization. Barely thirty square miles total area. Black-tailed deer and harbor seals.

"Wilma agrees with your uncle," he said.

"Merely a working hypothesis."

"She thinks wolves have been living out there all along. What do you think?"

"My father hunted the islands. He never saw them."

Old grief, like the prick of a thistle pressed in a book.

"Know a man named Hentov?"

"Ed, yes."

"He reliable?"

"My father hunted with him."

He turned to the woman. "There."

"Coyotes can't be ruled out," she admitted. "Dogs either, for that matter."

"Round up the usual suspects."

The woman laughed as if this were a witty thing to say. Caroline didn't get it.

She went about her work while they lingered over their drinks. From time to time she saw him write on a note pad. Their smiles came easily, then their yawns. He picked up the tab and left a twenty-percent tip — a sure sign he had been a long time out of state.

She followed them to the lobby and watched through the panel lights of the front door. They shook hands and he got into the Volkswagen and the woman got into the Land Cruiser. His lights came on, his horn beeped, he drove away. She beeped back, her lights came on, but she stayed put. After a minute she made a U-turn and drove down toward the marina. The street ended at the pier and there was no other way out of town. Caroline waited but the Land Cruiser did not swing back.

Later, after the crowd had dwindled to a few serious drinkers, she left Manly in charge and went to her room. She took off her skirt and shoes and put on jeans and boots, and bundled up in her parka and mittens and tassled cap and went out the back door. The cold pricked her eyes with pins. She walked to the marina and found the Land Cruiser at the pier but the woman was not in sight. She made her way along the sea wall to the jetty. The harbor light came round and she saw someone out on the rocks. When the light came round again the person was closer. She hid in the steep darkness at the entrance to the quarry and waited. The woman came by making b-r-r-r noises and talking to herself. She went along up the sea wall and soon a car door closed and an engine started and tires crunched on snow and then it was quiet. Caroline stepped out of the shadows and climbed the old quarry railbed. She faced the islands, strung along the bay and silver in the moonlight, lumpy, like a body under a sheet.

What was the woman looking for? The islands were miles away. Listening for? Caroline slowed her heart and listened between beats.

Daddy?

10

THE weekend crew, half as large and energetic as the regular staff, was getting around to putting together the Monday edition between reading the Sunday papers and making doughnut runs to the bakery around the corner. Only Angela worked with her usual weekday intensity. She was constantly on the move, perpetually in motion, in a loose red top and tight black slacks, and whenever Fran looked in her direction, his eyes snared by the sway of her breasts or the squirm of her hips, she would glance up or behind or around, catch him in the act, and smile.

Fran felt great ambivalence toward Angela. He wanted her and he didn't want her. If she had been healthy he would have had her by now. He wasn't afraid of cancer, but of the potential for tragic complications. What if she fell in love and he didn't? Imagine trying to dump a girl who could be dying. What if he fell in love and she did die? No thanks, divorce had been death enough.

She came waddling over to his desk. "Hey, Fran, what'cha working on?" Her face rocked back and forth in an excess of animation. Maybe she had always overdone it.

"My Steel Harbor story."

"See anything yesterday?"

"Nope."

"So what can you say?"

"That I didn't see anything, but in a creative way."

"Bullshit, huh?"

" 'Fraid so."

"Mr. Neville isn't going to like it."

"Poor Mr. Neville."

She grinned with mischievous delight, so broadly that he saw the skull beneath the skin. Pretty smile, gorgeous body, quick mind, good natured, and big hearted — it was almost as if the disease had a sense of the dramatic.

His phone rang.

"*Republic.*"

"How are we feeling today?"

"Hi, Wilma. Sore as hell. How about you?"

"I limbered up this morning with some yoga. Of course, I'm a runner so that helps."

He cupped his hand over the mouthpiece and asked Angela to go down to the morgue and see if she could dig up anything recent on coyotes in Maine. She pantomimed astonishment. In Maine? She saluted and started for the stairs, her leg brace forcing her to walk with a hitch that exaggerated the swing of her hips. Or was she playing that up, too?

Wilma said she had a positive identification on the skull they found the day before. The orbital angle and spherical characteristics of the auditory bullae confirmed it to be a wolf's. She couldn't date it, except to say that it was at least a hundred years old. A colleague suggested that the high salt content of the clay where it was found contributed to the remarkable state of preservation.

"Would it be strong enough to use as a weapon?"

"Give me an example."

"Could you beat somebody to death with it?"

"My goodness, Fran, I couldn't tell you. The bone is very hard, semi-petrified, but there's no trace of blood or recent fracture to indicate it might have been used that way."

"Don't mind me, I'm playing crime reporter."

"What a gruesome notion to be planting in my head right before I go back."

"When?"

"This afternoon. I'm going to establish an observation post near where we found the skull. The passage between the islands makes a natural runway."

He asked how long she planned to stay.

"Most of the week if I have to. You can't tell about these things. I may not see a thing the whole time or I could get lucky tonight."

She sounded more certain than she had the night before. He

wondered if hope had ripened to delusion or if she were holding something back.

"What do you know that I don't?"

She didn't answer right away. "I went down to the harbor last night after you left."

"I would have gone with you."

"It was an impulse. I didn't know myself until you drove away. I went out on the jetty. You can see the islands from there. I listened a long time, and at one point I'm sure I heard howling. At least three individuals. They seemed to communicate with each other from different locations. Fran, the wounds we saw on the doe were not inflicted by dogs."

"If you're right, are you going to be safe out there?"

"Wolves find biologists particularly unappetizing."

He reminded her of what happened to Sam Comstock.

Wolves were not above scavenging when the opportunity presented itself. They ate things dead they wouldn't ordinarily kill for food, including each other. That reminded her. What was the name of the doctor who examined the body? Tagen, yes, she had to ask him about those wounds. And Fran was not to worry. Her colleague would be out to check on her from time to time. Right now she had to get to the IGA and pick up some sardines. Wolves were crazy for sardines. They could smell them miles away.

She was in high spirits and full of plans and he restrained himself from being a worrywart and saying all the worrywart things.

"Wish me luck."

"Break a leg."

He felt uneasy after hanging up, like he wanted to do two things at once but didn't know what either of those things was so he did nothing. He was still at loose ends when Angela placed a clutch of photostats and clippings in front of him.

The coyote had turned up in Maine during the early seventies, sparking a feud between hunters and environmentalists that still raged. The hunters demanded bounties and predicted a blood bath that would lay waste the state's deer population. Environmentalists called this nonsense. Coyotes were respectable, well-mannered members of the ecological community. There was heated debate over the baby stealing issue, with hunters taking the view that a coyote liked nothing better than to steal a baby out of its stroller and drag it off to the den for breakfast. Environmentalists were as indignant over this as if a close friend's name had been dragged through the mud. They threatened lawsuits and slung a little mud themselves.

It was hard to believe the two groups were talking about the same creature. Photographs showed a hardy animal about half-way between a timber wolf and a scraggy, badlands coyote. It did not look like a fearsome killing machine. On the other hand, a certain lean and hungry look about the eyes and snout indicated that it probably would not make a suitable baby-sitter. Why such a fuss over a wild dog?

He thought he saw an answer in one of the photographs, the first picture taken of a Maine coyote, the first proof such a thing existed. The animal had been shot by a hunter in the Allagash country and strung up like an outlaw surrounded by a posse of men with rifles. The animal's eyes were squeezed shut and the mouth hung lax with a strip of tongue like flypaper hanging out. The men posed tough. One man kicked at the dirt as if it were a coyote's hide — or an environmentalist's. Another man spit at the animal. Who in his right mind would spit at a dead animal? That was exactly the point. The men were not in their right minds. The coyote had brought out the coyote in them.

"Something wrong?" Angela said. She'd been watching him.

"Wilma — Professor Swanson — is going back to the islands tonight."

Angela's brow worked in thought. "She'd tell you first if she found anything, wouldn't she?"

He said yes.

"So what's to worry?"

11

HOW quiet it was. She had never heard such silence. It was loud between breaths. She heard the crackle of ice crystals as the temperature fell. She heard the air sigh in the chambers of her air mattress when she moved. She heard the ping of the second hand of her quartz watch as it crept along the graphite face. Then she didn't. She reached down into her sleeping bag and pulled out a small flashlight and shone it on the watch. It had stopped: 12:16 A.M.

She lay propped on an elbow facing the door flap of her backpacker tent, chin resting in the palm of her hand, fully dressed except for her boots, sleeping bag drawn up like a comforter. Beyond the opening was a windbreak of piled snow and spruce boughs. She had rigged a blind in front with a gap to mount her tripod and camera. The tripod was set, the camera and flash protected by a drawstring hood. The silvery ovals of sardines and the silvery rectangles of their oily tins were strewn across the spit in a line from the dead hemlock tree to the observation post. The sardines had long since frozen but she could still smell them. The smell hung in the breezeless, stingy air and on her hands.

A wolf comes and licks up the sardines by the tree and licks its way across the snow like the birds pecking up the bread left by Hansel and sticks its head into the tent and licks her fingers with a rough tongue.

"Steady," she said out loud. It was good hearing the sound of her own voice in the dark. It gave her a center.

Moonlight and starlight on the snow were all brightness against the darkness inside the tent. The bleak trunk and branches of the hemlock rose at an angle above the stunted treetops like the mast of a foundered ship. There was something in the tree. Her flashlight wouldn't reach. The raven? She squinted and couldn't tell. She opened her eyes so wide she felt rings of pressure around the edges. She couldn't tell. Ravens were rarely about at night. How about an owl? Her mind liked the idea but her eyes told her it wasn't an owl. They told her just that much.

She stared into the darkness of the tent, allowing her pupils to dilate fully, then looked again. Now she saw the object hanging from the tree instead of sitting in it. The object had lengthened, and it swayed, like the doe in the barn. A classic example of hallucination caused by sensory deprivation. She would not let herself be fooled. She simply would not look.

A short time later she heard howling. One, two, three animals. Two were far out on the islands, but one was in the woods of the first island near the ice bridge. They were not hallucinations. She removed the hood from the camera. She had no infrared equipment, and that could mean only one shot before the flash sent the animals fleeing back into the woods. The howling came again, closer all around. Coyotes, her eye. These were the cries of wolves. She could tell by the timbre, the range in pitch, the extensiveness of the repertoire. She distinguished as many as half a dozen individuals. This surprised her because the Channel Islands could not have exceeded Coronation Island in total area, and there the pack never numbered more than four adults. She must make a note.

Patience. She always had plenty of it, had practiced it, used it to get what she wanted. Now she had none. Her mind spun out of control. One thought bumped into the next. Images blurred past like box cars. She fretted. She fretted that the scent of the sardines would not carry, that wolves operating so close to civilization would be too wary to show, that the camera would fail. She checked it and, fretful she might have fouled it in checking, checked it again.

She was aware of a terrible smell, like a fat man's fart, like his stale cigars. The mud flats at low tide reeked even in winter, but the odor was more complex, more evil, than just that. It was like sulfur, like gunpowder, burning sewage. Smells had once been thought to carry disease. Another instance of reason fooled by the senses. Effect masquerading as cause. Until Pasteur proved otherwise. Often in her work she imagined the master looking over her shoulder. How would he have proceeded? What would he have done? The brave thing, certainly. The direct thing. Tonight he would have heartily approved of her methodology. He was a hands-on scientist. Like when he took samples of sputum directly from the snapping jaws of hydrophobic dogs.

A sound like a baby's whimper came from the nearby woods. They were here.

She detected activity at the woodline. Brush crackled. Claws scraped the crust. A yip, a snort, then a yawning snarl was rolled deep in the throat until cut off abruptly by a snap of teeth. All at once there was a terrible uproar: biting, ripping, screaming; growls and howls and unearthly laughter. It sounded like a pack fight, as if order had broken down and all the pack members had laid into each other. Most horrible of all was a gurgling, choking sound that trilled and hoarsened the others, a gasping, phlegmy, congested wheeze. This could not be. Wolf society was usually harmonious. Unless . . .

She turned the flashlight on the woodline and brought to light a roiling gnarl of unkempt fur and bright fangs and eyes strangely red in the weak, yellow beam. The struggle stopped, the animals let go their neighbors' throats and looked as one into the eye of the light. There were eight or more, with feverish eyes and snouts crinkled back in grins that bared shiny black gums and fangs that dribbled foam.

Rabies.

The observer became a pair of eyes. The she they were connected to, the center, was gone. The eyes saw the creatures untangle themselves and start to come. The flashlight dropped from the hand. The eyes saw a triangle of blackness outside the revolving brightness of the tent as the flashlight rolled to a stop in the corner and shone on a brass eyelet at the base of the door flap. The dark aperture ringed by bright brass was a mousehole to another universe. Perhaps the she was hiding there.

The hands knew there was work to be done. They aimed the camera and shot the first picture. The flash illuminated the approaching creatures so briefly it froze their motion. They did not seem to be moving but they were closer. The image died away almost as soon as it was born, leaving streaks that had been teeth, eyes, and legs stabbing forward. The clever, autonomous hands reset the camera. The ears noted the ping of the recharger, the eyes another blinding, illuminating flash. The creatures appeared again, frozen, no sign of movement except that their distance from the tent had halved, like a game of 1-2-3 Redlight played by murderous children.

In the blackness that followed, the ears could not make out the camera sounds because of the animal sounds. There was wheezing and groaning and clacking, and something else, a sound like a siren far away in a nighttime city, only it came from inside, deep inside and rising. The able hands were ready. The night flashed bright on the gap jammed with paws, ears, eyes, snouts, teeth, tongues, bristles, and satin-black gums. Bubbles of froth reflected the flash like strings of pearls. As bright went black and spider webs of flash pulsed before the eyes, the ears heard the siren come round corners and down back streets, closer, shatteringly loud. They heard the scream even after the physical act of screaming was made impossible by the severing of the vocal cords when the throat was torn out. Until the thunderclap snap of the neck.

12

ANOTHER unremembered dream. Not being able to remember meant not being able to forget. He couldn't put it behind him. Threat hung over him like the cold spell that hung over the land.

The dawn sky was hazy and light came through pale and meager from no place in particular. His car looked like it would never move again. Stalactites of dirty ice hung from the fenders and welded them to the curb. Across the street Jimmy in shirt sleeves and earmuffs sprinkled sand on the sidewalk in front of the market. Next door, Mrs. Connors, the cat lady, wrapped in shawls like a gypsy, let some of her kitties in and some out. In the schoolyard down the block the snow came over the seats of the swings so all that showed were the chains. Fran looked at these things without seeing them. He was seeing California.

He saw Leo Carrillo Beach north of Malibu. He felt the sun that was warm through November and the buoyant, green-blue, high rolling sea that exhilarated but never chilled. He heard the children shrieking in the sea caves and smelled the oiled women. He saw Susan slim in her electric-blue maillot cut high at the thigh. How he wanted her now, when all his world was ice.

He walked to work instead of taking the car. He needed the fresh air and exercise and the extra time. Outside the *Republic* building he met Ray and they said good morning and went upstairs together. Neither said a thing after good morning. Ray got them some coffee.

"Come on down to the fishbowl," he said.

When they were inside he closed the door and looked out across the newsroom at Tommy Blackburn's vacant desk. "Jean Claude isn't back from the slopes, I see. He did a good piece Friday before he left. Read it?"

Fran said he had.

"I bet you did. I bet you did because you wrote it."

Fran didn't know what to say. Ray did.

"From now on, it's your story. Get what he has and take it from there. Wait a minute, wait a minute, let me talk to him first. In the meantime see what Angela has." Pause. "Well?"

"I left L.A. to get away from this sort of thing, Ray."

"You know what they say about California. It's the future of everyplace else."

Fran went down to the morgue where Angela was busy cutting up the morning paper and hiding the clippings. She had on a close-fitting, plum-colored corduroy jumper that made her look schoolgirlish and eager. She gave him a smile nobody had any business giving anybody else at work.

"New assignment," he said.

"That makes three at once."

"Ray wants you to help."

How quickly she put aside her other work for him. He was still angry at Ray and it was an easy matter to include her.

"What's our new assignment?"

"Tommy's."

He watched to see how she took it. She made a resigned, comic-sad face. A cartoon face. He could have slapped it.

"It had to happen sooner or later," she said. "Everybody knew."

"Did everybody know I'd be the one to make it happen?"

Finally. A little light went on — or out. She saw how it stood with him. Then, no twinkly eye, no perky grin, no spunky stiff-upper-lip stuff. "You see through me. That's why I make you cross."

The anger went out of him, and as if that had been the only thing holding him up, he slumped in the chair by the desk.

"Remember a character in *Li'l Abner* who went around with dark storm clouds over his head?"

"I can look it up."

He smiled in frustration. "What I mean is I feel like him. I feel a

I 68 I

sense of impending doom. I felt it in California. It got so bad I had to leave. I thought I left it there but it's caught up to me and there's no place to go from here." He became reckless. "What do you do? You have it worse. How do you handle it?"

Probably no one had ever asked her such a question, the etiquette of cancer demanding that victim and well-wisher stay clear of the abyss.

"I try not the think about it," she said.

"But when you do, what do you think?"

"I remember things, things that made me happy. We lived in Fort Lauderdale my first two years of high school. I think about my friends there, my boyfriend, sailing. Sometimes . . ." She stopped.

"Sometimes?"

"Sometimes I have dirty thoughts, really amazing ones."

"But when nostalgia and eroticism don't work, what gets you through the night?"

She had no answer.

"God?" he said.

"I say the *Hail Mary,* but I don't know if anybody's listening. It's just sort of a comfort."

What did he expect? Hope wrought from despair? Spiritual renewal from the harrowing of the flesh? Something ennobling in suffering? Perhaps there was, but it was nothing she could impart, at least not there, then, and most importantly, without his love.

She had been leaning back on her hands against the desk and before he knew what he was doing he reached out and placed the palm of his hand on the point of her blighted hip. The hand moved up and down the wales of corduroy and massaged her wound. He felt the atrophied thigh in contrast to its plump opposite. He felt — not so much felt as intuited by touch — the nubby scars of stitches and gougings of biopsies, the violations of scalpel, hypodermic, and catheter. He wanted to be her lightning rod. He wanted to conduct the pain away from her, take it all away and make her safe. She trembled beneath his hand in a swoon of pleasure.

The phone rang. They drew apart. It rang again. Fran felt exactly as he would if an alarm had awakened him from a deep sleep. Angela groped for the phone as if she had been asleep with him. She picked up the receiver and listened. "Mr. Neville," she said, and handed it to him.

"Edna Sergeant's on my line, Fran," Ray said. "I'm going to roll her over to you."

Click.

"Ray?" said a woman's voice, breathless.

"This is Fran."

"Fran?"

"Yes, Edna, what is it?"

"They've found another body. A woman's. She's been decapitated."

13

WAS it possible, ever, for a man and woman to understand one another? Was there ever any real connecting? Why were relationships, even the longest lived, so incomplete? Fran thought of these things on the drive down to Steel Harbor. Wilma's death had made him think of his divorce, but in a new way. It seemed to him that the pain, the deception, the chaos, the helplessness (especially the helplessness — everybody thinking he was a victim and nobody wrong) were all part of the universal state of human relationships and not peculiar to divorce. He saw all over again Wilma kneeling by the dead doe, blood smeared to her forehead, her vulnerable eyes looking up into his. What had she wanted? What had he to give?

Today Steel Harbor was anything but a seacoast village hibernating its way through winter. Police and other official cars lined the curbs, and when he turned off his engine in front of the Town Building he heard the drone of another high above, the airborne wing of the task force. He went inside and found Caroline Parker alone on the bench outside the chief's office. Her eyes were glazed over with the look people get waiting on benches outside offices.

"They have Uncle Woody," she said.

"Arrested?"

"They won't tell me. Can you hear what they're saying?"

He wanted to help her. He wanted to be more than a reporter to her. It had something to do with Wilma's death. He made out voices and the squawk of a short-wave radio on the other side of the door, but before he could do any serious eavesdropping, two state troopers in fur caps came in from the street. They stamped snow off their boots and agreed that so-and-so was a horse's ass. They clammed up when they saw Caroline. The chief's door opened and the voices and squawking got louder. Fran saw a man in street clothes and a crewcut sitting behind the desk. The chief stood in the background looking displaced.

"Mal?" Caroline said.

The chief said something to the plainclothesman and stepped outside. "Woody's safe and sound," he told her. "These people know their business. They're going by the book. It'll work out, I promise."

"Work out for who?" she said.

"Hey, I'm on your side. I don't think Woody had a thing to do with Professor Swanson's death."

Caroline's eyes widened. "They think he did it?"

"We don't think anything for sure. All we know is that she parked in the turnout out by the springs and must have passed his cabin on her way to the islands. He refuses to cooperate, and you know as well as I do that nobody goes by there without him knowing about it. The worst of it is he came near laying open one of these people's heads with his ax."

"Bullies," Caroline said. "You scared him. Who wouldn't be scared with a bunch of bullies ganging up?"

"He made it hard on himself and now he has to go to Riverston. You'd do well to find him a lawyer."

"When can I see him?"

"Get Paul Nadeau over here and I'll see to it you both see him."

Fran watched her go, graceful but not especially feminine, a childlike grace. There was something unformed or held back about Caroline Parker. The way she expressed herself, the way she carried herself. Her downy, perfect skin and nascent breasts contributed to the impression, an overall softness without heaviness, as if the last layer of baby fat had never been burned off in the heat of adolescence. She's a virgin, he thought. Even if she isn't, she is.

"Guess I was wrong," Mal said. He was in no hurry to go back into the office full of troopers.

"About what?"

"Never heard of dogs doing a thing like this."

A muscle twitched in Fran's jaw. "Edna Sergeant says the body was decapitated."

"Head lying there like a bowling ball. Damn crows pecked out her eyes."

Wilma's soulful eyes — bird food. Fran had to distance himself, for his own sake as well as for his job. "Chopped off?" he said, thinking of Woody's ax, anything to foster the illusion of professional invulnerabilty.

"More like hacked. Or chewed."

"I thought you ruled out dogs."

"I did."

"Wolves?"

Mal watched the door to his office. "Off the record?"

"Sure."

"If it's a wolf it's a two-legged one."

"You mean a maniac or something like that?"

Mal watched the door.

"Who found her?"

"Fellow from the university. Went out to check on her this morning. She was staying out there in a tent."

"Her observation post."

The chief gave him a look.

"She told me she was going."

"Funny how you keep coming up with particulars."

"Think I'm your maniac?"

The chief didn't say.

"Where's the guy who found her?"

"Over to Sergeant's with the body. Seemed about half dead himself."

"Thanks for talking to me." Fran was feeling better, stronger. He almost believed that he was what he did and not what he was.

"Mind if I ask if she was anything to you?" the chief said. "I mean more than just somebody you were working with."

"We didn't have time. Saturday was the first we met."

"And the last?"

"And the last."

From the Town Building Fran went up the street to the funeral home. An ambulance was parked out front. Before he had a chance to pull the bell lever, Edna Sergeant opened the door.

"I saw you from the window. Albert is with Dr. Tagen and the medical examiner downstairs. We lesser lights are not admitted."

"Are they doing the autopsy?"

"I think the plan is to transport the remains to Riverston. That explains the presence of these gentlemen."

Two men in hospital whites under heavy coats were waiting in the near parlor. Beyond them in a second parlor another man sat by himself. He was dressed in outdoor gear — the latest and the best. His face, framed by a trim, black beard, was shockingly pale.

"Professor Phillip Hallahan of Orono," Mrs. Sergeant said. "Come, I'll introduce you."

Hallahan stood as they approached. He seemed unsure of his legs and held on to the back of the chair. Mrs. Sergeant said Fran was a friend who worked for the *Republic.*

"I'm a reporter," Fran said, answering the question he saw in Hallahan's eyes. They were horribly tortured eyes, black-Irish and despairing.

"Wilma told me about you." The way he said it made Fran think that Wilma and Hallahan had been more than colleagues. It was just like Wilma to refer to her lover as a colleague. Careful, he thought.

"Are you a biologist, too?"

"My field is applied genetics. Stock improvement, immunology, that sort of thing." Hallahan seemed relieved to be able to talk shop.

"Did Wilma show you the skull she found?"

"As a matter of fact she asked me to verify her findings."

"A wolf's?"

"Definitely."

"She seemed to think there might still be some around." As

Fran approached the subject they both knew he must, Hallahan began avoiding his eyes. "Could they have killed her?"

"Not my field."

"How about the wounds? You must have seen livestock killed by animals. Wouldn't that be your field?"

"Look, I've been through all this with the Keystone Kops over there. Go ask them. She was butchered. She was meat. What can I say?"

"You can say what you really think."

Hallahan attempted a smile, a gruesome affair that was more like the grin of pain. "She would have said no, wolves couldn't possibly have done it," he said, morosely equivocal, torturing himself with some secret regret. "I used to tell her that wolves were her surrogate children."

"Funny," Fran said. "I thought that, too."

The two men looked at one another.

Edna Sergeant interrupted. "Quick, the game is afoot."

The men in whites had left. Fran reached the door in time to see the ambulance sink stern-first below the drive at the side of the house. He crossed the deep snow of the lawn to the terrace wall and looked down on Mr. Sergeant in shirt sleeves and a bloody apron directing the ambulance in close to the ramp at the lower entryway. The men opened the back of the van and went into the building. Fran walked down the drive and waited. After a while the door opened and the men wheeled out a gurney and transferred the body bag on it into the ambulance. Dr. Tagen and a round-faced man in glasses followed. Last out was Mr. Sergeant, buttoning his coat, straightening his tie.

"Darn her," he said when he saw Fran.

Fran asked the round-faced man if he were from the medical examiner's office. The man's glasses were very powerful and his eyes bulged like a frog's when he looked right at you.

"I'm Dr. Brower. I *am* the medical examiner."

"A reporter, sir," Mr. Sergeant said.

Fran talked fast. He had been working with the deceased, had spoken to her the previous day, knew her plans. Sometimes the best way to get information was to give it. Brower was interested.

"Drop by the hospital tomorrow."

"Have you completed the autopsy?"

"Only the prelim." A significant look at Dr. Tagen, who, it seemed to Fran, was extremely uncomfortable. "Much remains to be done."

"Do you have a cause of death yet?"

The eyes bulged and the lips compressed in a slim grin. "Tomorrow."

The ambulance pulled away, the exhaust slithering like blue snakes along the icy pavement. The two doctors and the undertaker were already on their way indoors.

"Dr. Tagen," Fran said before Mr. Sergeant could close the door.

The old doctor, stooped yet towering over the other two, turned halfway around, showing an avian profile and one dull eye.

"Did Wilma Swanson get to talk to you yesterday? She told me she wanted to."

The eye darted, pulling that whole side of the face out of line. "Never saw her. I wish . . . I wish . . . ." He didn't finish.

"Satisfied?" Mr. Sergeant said. He steered the old man inside and shut the door with firmness, leaving Fran alone on the suddenly deserted drive.

"No," he shouted. His voice echoed off the clapboards like a shot.

14

THE empty Land Cruiser was wedged between two empty police cars. A dozen other cars, pickups, and flatbeds were parked along the road. Everything was hush. It was the time of mildness before the onset of winter night. As Fran walked down through the woods he began hearing the buzz of snowmobiles and the distant shouts of men. Tracks crisscrossed the snow in every direction. In the meadow two machines caught him from behind and whizzed past. The drivers were boys. They grinned back at him and at each other and jumped the drift that covered the springs. After they and their noise disappeared into the trees he heard an airplane. A fish-and-game ski Cessna banked low over the estuary. He did not hear the gurgle of the hidden water.

A trooper in sunglasses was talking to a civilian on the steps of Woody's cabin. The civilian was drinking a can of root beer. The pull-tab lay on the snow at his feet. Fran went inside. A detective in a trench coat was handling Woody's traps and making coments to a trooper in jackboots and breeches stretched out in Woody's rocker. Mal Boulding's deputy tended the stove. He had caught a chill.

Fran asked if he had been to the islands.

"Been dickin' round out there since morning," he said.

"See the body?"

"See it? I got stuck guarding it while Mal went back and called the staties."

The trooper in front of the fire scowled, his clean-shaven jowls plumped out like a mastiff's.

"You could do some hurt with this one," the detective said, hefting the wolf trap. He was short and barrel-chested with a short man's cockiness, and in the trench coat he looked like Napoleon. "You could spring it on your victim or use the jaws to strike with. That would explain the tooth marks, wouldn't you say so, Carl?"

"Yes, sir," the trooper said, pulling in his legs and sitting up at attention like a good dog.

"We better bring this trap in with the ax and let the lab have a look."

Carl was all for it.

Fran asked the deputy what he thought.

"Ain't paid enough to think." He meant it as a joke but nobody laughed. "It's a animal," he added. "Don't see how any man, even a luniac, could mess up a woman like that." He shivered and held his hands flat to the stove. He just couldn't get warm.

"Wouldn't they have found an animal by now?"

"You don't find what you don't look for," the deputy said. "They're sweeping for weapons with a metal detector. They even broke into Ed Hentov's boathouse. That's private property."

"We called in on that," said the trooper in sunglasses. He had just come inside.

"What's Hentov's line of work?" Fran said. He remembered Wilma's encounter with the hunter.

The deputy acted surprised an educated fellow like Fran didn't know about Ed Hentov. "Bigwig over to Tidewater Paper, don't you know?"

Paper companies were hungry for land and thirsty for fresh water. "He own much property out there?"

The deputy smiled. "You reporters. Just like hound dogs, ain't you? Always sniffing."

The other policemen did not smile. They looked at Fran like three roosters that had just discovered a weasel in the hen house. The wolf trap slipped into the folds of the trench coat. The drag chain clinked.

After a moment of stifling silence the detective spoke — not to Fran but to the deputy. "You mean you let the press in here without warning us? I thought he was one of yours."

"So did I," said the trooper in breeches.

"I don't see the harm."

"He doesn't see the harm," said the trooper in sunglasses.

"What paper you work for?" the detective said.

Fran told him.

"I know your boss over there, Ray Neville. Good man. I don't think he'd be real happy to hear that one of his people was going around asking questions without ID-ing himself."

"Ray taught me everything I know."

"Why am I wasting my time with this guy?"

"Beats me," said the trooper in breeches.

The trooper in sunglasses opened the door.

15

BY the time Fran got back to Steel Harbor it was twilight, a rosy twilight that cast the big white houses in glimmering pink. The snow squeaked under foot as the temperature fell. A small crowd huddled against the cold outside the Town Building. There were reporters from as far away as Boston and a Portland TV news team. The bits of conversation — it was all in bits, nobody spoke in sentences or stuck to a subject — ran from shop talk to speculation about the story. Fran was glad he was the new kid on the block and nobody knew him by sight. If it had gotten around that he had broken the original story, his brother and sister journalists would have turned on him like a pack of dogs on one of their own that has come by a large, meaty bone.

An unmarked car driven by a sheriff's deputy pulled up and the TV news people with a videotape-pack unit shoved their way to the curb. The door of the Town Building opened and Woody Parker stepped outside flanked by a second sheriff's deputy and the plainclothesman with the crewcut. Behind them came Caroline and a jaundiced-looking man with skin as yellow as his camel hair coat. Woody's wild, trapped eyes darted down the gauntlet of reporters and cameras. He shrank back and his escorts had to push him forward. Questions were hurled like insults. Flashes popped off in the dusk like gunfire. The video flood came on, flattening faces and lengthening shadows, and the smartly tailored, impeccably coifed TV news personality thrust a microphone in Woody's face. "Did you do it? Did you do it? How do you feel?" Woody flinched like Lee Harvey Oswald that day in Dallas.

Fran looked on from the other side of the waiting car. He saw Woody's frantic eyes and Caroline's dry lips bitten with worry. He saw the iron-faced cops betray sparks of hatred as they pushed back the press, and the press itself, surging, milling, posturing, creating the event by covering it. The worst thing that could happen to a hermit, his worst nightmare, surely as harrowing as the torment of wolves real or imagined, had happened to Woody. He had become a public figure, had brought notice to himself by so strenuously, so noticeably, trying to avoid it.

The rear door of the car was locked, and the plainclothesman yelled to the driver. During the delay Woody glanced over the hood at Fran, and in a voice barely audible above all the noise, said, "Think you know something, do you? S-S-Study the winter of '24 in your newspaper and you'll know something for sure." The door was unlocked and Woody got inside. The plainclothesman eyed Fran. Caroline looked at him, too, with the look of a woman forced to depend on a man she doesn't trust.

You will not let me down, a command; *Will you?* a question.

The car Woody was in pulled away. Caroline and the yellow-faced man got into another and followed. Mal Boulding stood on the steps and fielded questions. He wan't saying anything Fran didn't already know, except Wilma's age, thirty-eight, and that the search party was due back shortly. He drifted across the street to the inn. With a reporter's knack for noting the location of telephones, he remembered a pay phone outside the taproom.

Angela was ready. He relayed the facts, spelling out names and underscoring highlights so she could write the story by deadline. He heard her rapid typing, her throaty breath. When he was through she read it back.

"One last thing, Angie. Do we have back copies of the paper to 1924?"

"On microfilm. What'cha looking for?"

"I won't know until I see it."

He heard Ray's voice in the background. Mr. Neville wanted to know when he was coming in, she said. He told her he was going to hang around until the search party got back. He heard her tell Ray and Ray say something. Mr. Neville wanted to see him in the morning about his other assignments. He wanted to see him early.

"Tell Mr. Neville . . . Tell him good night."

Fran went into the taproom and ordered a beer. Mrs. Parker was filling in for Caroline in an exasperated, put-upon sort of way, as if the main reason Woody had gotten into trouble was to deprive the inn of his niece's services, thereby forcing Mrs. Parker to cover for her. Fran had come to think of the woman as the wicked stepmother in a fairy tale. Who did that make Caroline — Cinderella? Sleeping Beauty? Who did that make him?

Prince Charming was trying to decide whether to risk a second beer on an empty stomach when he heard car doors banging and men shouting on the street. The door burst open and the taproom filled with men. The chief's deputy was the only policeman. Pitchers and shots were set up. After a day chafing under the supervision of the state police they were like kids out of school.

Fran order the second beer and listened. He listened to the bragging and complaining, the jokes, the interminable arguments. One argument was about who found the camera. He stepped to the bar and introduced himself to the man who most vehemently claimed he had.

"One of them expensive jobs that look old-fashioned," he said when Fran asked him about it.

"35-millimeter."

"That's it. Had a flash that didn't need bulbs. State cop said an outfit like that could run as much as a boat and motor."

Fran asked what had happened to it, but before the man could answer the deputy broke in. "You hadn't ought to be talking to that fella," he said, still smarting from his own garrulity earlier. "He's the press."

"I know who he is." The man darted a defiant squint at the deputy, ready to do battle for Fran's First Amendment rights. "That camera was took into Mal's office not a hour ago."

Fran bought a round for the deputy and the man who found the camera and went across the street. The out-of-town police and press were gone. The chief's door was open a crack with a wedge of light spilled into the dark corridor. He knocked and looked inside. Mal sat with his feet up on the desk in a clutter of dirty ashtrays and styrofoam cups. He waved Fran in.

"All gone?" Fran said.

"All gone."

"Did your deputy tell you what happened at Woody's?"

"I heard."

"Hope I didn't cause trouble."

"We all have our hats to wear."

Fran asked about the camera.

"And you're wearing your reporter hat and want to know if the film was exposed. You want to know if it's being developed. You want to know if you can have a look when it is. Commendable. You are doing your job. We are all doing our jobs. And that fine woman is dead."

He placed his index fingers on either side of his nose and massaged the darkened, baggy flesh beneath his eyes. "I should have something in a couple days."

"Thanks, Mal. I'll try to leave my reporter hat at home."

"Don't kid youself," he said. "It's nailed on. They all are."

16

THE squeak of the car door in the dry cold set his teeth on edge and the freezing vinyl seat cover made his thighs feel wet. First came the *roh-roh-roh* of the starter, then the engine popped to life with a peppy grumble. He pulled on the lights, dim then brightening as the VW lurched out of its frozen ruts. The headlamps showed parked cars along the street, reflectors winking back red and yellow. At the crossroads they shone on the clapboards of the funeral home. Then cars and houses fell away until white road rolled through black trees along the lonely stretch of woods between Steel Harbor and Riverston.

The windshield fogged over. The defroster was not much help so he cleared the glass with his hand and left a filmy streak that made him feel like a goldfish looking out of its bowl. He took what appeared to be an easy curve, but the watery glass deceived him and he had to turn sharply. A funny thing happened to the lights. They floated across the road into the boughs of the pine trees. There was a thump, like being hit in the back of the head with a pillow, and the car stopped. Glistening pine needles reflected the steady, slanting beam of the headlights. Then the lights went dead.

The engine died, too. He turned off the ignition and turned it on. Nothing. He pulled the lights on and off a few times. No response. He got out and took a look. The rear bumper was stuck in the snowbank, but there didn't seem to be any damage. The rear wheels were buried to the hubs in the soft snow of the shoulder with the front of the car nosing the driving lane. No one was coming. He couldn't decide whether to stay with the car or walk back to town. Then he thought of something very frightening. He looked down the starlit road and at the black woods pressing on either side and he thought of how Sam Comstock and Wilma Swanson had died and that whoever or whatever had killed them might on such a night and in such a place kill again.

He got into the car and pressed the locks on both doors. He made sure nothing was hiding in the back.

After a while headlights appeared from the direction of Riverston. They came around the other side of the curve that had been his undoing and bathed the stranded car in light. He got out and waved the rig down, a four-wheel-drive Blazer. The driver's side window was lowered. "Been here long?" The driver was Ed Hentov.

Fran went around and climbed into the cab. The sudden warmth gave him a chill. Hentov looked down on the moon-colored roof of the VW.

"Looks like you'll need that tow after all."

"She's dead," Fran said. "Professor Swanson's dead."

"How'd it happen?" Hentov didn't sound surprised.

"Like Sam Comstock."

Hentov zipped up his parka and pulled the wolf-hair-trimmed hood over his head. "Let's have a look at your Beetle." He tried his hand at starting the car. When he couldn't, he backed the Blazer into position and hooked up the tow.

Fran got in behind the wheel of the VW. The Blazer pulled out, the cable stiffened. There was a zing, a crack, a moan of metal. The snowbank gave and the car moved under him. They rolled down the road toward town. With no motor noise he heard the tires crunch on the snow, the way a glider pilot hears the wind.

Before town they turned down a private road. An angular house with high, glowing windows rose from the gloom. They pulled up to a three-door garage and the nearest door swung open and the light came on. Hentov released the cable, drove round back, and nudged the little car inside. Beyond the Volvo station wagon in the next stall were snowmobiles, dirt bikes, boat and trailer, power tools of every sort. "I have two sons," Hentov said. "My wife says she has three."

They entered the house through a glass patio. Dog tags jangled and the husky trotted out to greet them. Fran had yet to hear this wolflike creature bark like a dog. They sized one another up.

Hentov led the way through the kitchen, all stainless steel and butcher block. The platformed dining and living rooms were carpeted in silver pile and furnished in chrome and glass. The white brick fireplace looked as if it had never been used. Hentov called out the name Barbara and winked at Fran. The wink said Barbara was his wife.

A trim, dark-haired woman in designer jeans and a floppy turtleneck appeared in the doorway across the room. She smoothed her hands down her hips as she approached the men and smiled uncertainly. She had brilliant Semitic eyes.

"You must be chilled to the bone," she said to Fran when introductions and explanations were over. She had a slight Long Island accent and a tonal clarity as intense as her eyes.

Hentov shed his parka. He was wearing business clothes underneath and Fran made noises about imposing. Nonsense, Hentov said, they'd have a bite to eat and tear into his Beetle and he'd be on his way in no time. They didn't have family meals most nights, anyway, Barbara put in. Ed worked so late. Besides, Fran didn't want to deprive Ed of the pleasure of getting grease under his fingernails. Hentov traded a kiss for this little barb and went upstairs to change. Barbara got Fran involved in making the coffee. She started from scratch and ground the beans fresh in one of the gleaming gismos on the kitchen counter. The aroma was unbelievably homey and roasty. It was a tradition with them when Ed worked late, she said.

She was one of the unhappiest people Fran had ever met.

They had their coffee in the kitchen with corned-beef sandwiches. Halfway through two boys wandered in. They found the deli paper parcel and threw back their heads like young robins and lowered the leftover strips of spicy meat into their mouths. The Hentov children were introduced to Fran. Eddy, in the throes of puberty and all elbows and Adam's apple, was dark like his mother. Barry, a pudgy and serious little boy, had his father's sandy hair and blue eyes. They were full of rumors from school about the dead lady found on the islands.

"Woody Parker did it," Eddy said. "Everybody says he's mental."

"I'm not so sure." Barry had his father's way of weighing his words as he spoke. "I wouldn't be surprised if Daddy's right."

"Pretty tall order for coyotes," Fran said to Ed.

"Not if they're rabid," Barry piped up.

Fran had a vision of Wilma two days before, munching trail mix and talking about Pasteur. He saw something else, too, hazy and shining, streaking, a smear of light. He and the husky exchanged glances.

"Don't mind him, Mr. Thomas," Eddy said, giving his brother a poke. "*Old Yeller* was on TV Sunday night."

Barbara wanted to know who the lady was and Fran explained.

"They think this retarded man murdered her?"

"Retarded," Eddy snickered.

Hentov's face clenched like a fist. "Woody Parker knows more about the woods than you or I ever will," he said to Eddy. "If he's retarded, what does that make us?"

"Mom said it."

"Don't talk like a coward."

"Ed."

Hentov got up from the table. "Fran's had a rough day. We're not making it easier."

Fran got up, too. He thanked Barbara for supper. She said how much they enjoyed having him. "We rarely entertain here in the country."

"Barb's a New York girl," Hentov said. "She misses the city lights."

Back in the garage Ed found the problem right away. The bolt that held the battery ground had sheared off from the pan. He had to drill a new bolt hole with a half-inch drill. Fran pretended to watch the work but he was really watching the man. Ed Hentov was in his forties, limber yet restrained, not handsome so much as ugly in a handsome way. The face was dominated by high cheek-bones that pinched the outer corners of the eyes and gave them a Slavic cast. The personality was dominated by a contradiction. Ed was patient, methodical, sure-handed — the sort who brought maturity to bear on any task he undertook. Yet how mature was hunting coyotes from a snowmobile?

"Now let's see if we've got something that'll fit."

Naturally he did. He had more nuts and bolts than a hardware store. Fran climbed into the back of the Bug and steadied the bolt while Ed disappeared into the gullet of the open hood and tightened it.

"Crank her up," he said, smiling through a grimy face.

Fran tried the ignition and the engine came to life. The lights worked, too. He backed out of the garage and rolled down the window as Hentov came over.

"I have to ask you something, Ed." Fran thought of what Mal Boulding had said about his reporter's hat — like a priest's stole — only the sins a reporter heard were neither held in confidence nor forgiven.

"I heard today that you own the boathouse on the islands."

Ed didn't say that he didn't.

"Mind my asking what else you own out there?"

"I do mind."

"I can find out on my own."

"That's the way it'll have to be. A Yankee never tells how much land he owns." Pause. "A Yankee never asks." Ed turned and went back inside the garage and the steel door dropped smoothly behind him.

Fran realized he hadn't exactly shown his gratitude. Touchy bastard, though. And this Yankee business. The man had no more Yankee accent than Fran, a decade out of state. And how many Yankees carried off Jewish princesses from New York, holing up in Frank Lloyd Wright–inspired strongholds and scanning a hostile terrain with Tartar eyes?

He turned down the winding drive that was more like a logging road than a driveway. The snowbanks on either side were as high as the roof of the car. Shaggy spruce trees craned over to get a better look as he passed. A final turn, the main road ahead, but just at the entrance his headlights came back at him in the eyes of a large animal standing in the middle of the lane. He hit the brake and horn at the same time and the animal leapt over the bank into the woods. The husky must have gotten out, he told himself as he turned onto Tidewater Road.

He didn't believe it for a minute.

17

THE first person Fran met next morning when he went to work was Tommy Blackburn. He met him in the men's room. Fran was standing at the urinal and heard the door open and Tommy stepped up to the next basin. Tommy stared at the tile wall. Fran said good morning.

"You asshole," Tommy said to the wall.

"How did I rate that?"

"For blabbing to Ray about writing my story for me last week."

"Did Ray tell you that?"

"He told me I was fired."

Both were silent as they finished and zipped up. They washed at the sinks. Now Tommy was staring into the mirror.

"I never said a thing to Ray."

They took paper towels from the dispenser and dried their hands. As Fran tried to leave Tommy grabbed him by the collar and shoved him against the wall. He pinned him across the throat with his forearm and cocked his right back in a fist.

"Me first," he said, and went for the door. He didn't make it.

Fran saw white. When he saw normally again he and Tommy were on the floor. Tommy was on top with his back to him and Fran had him in a strangle hold. Tommy tried to break the hold, but Fran had the powerful wrists of a rangy man whose strength came from leverage. He could have killed him. He wanted to. He felt Tommy's pulse against his own. He felt the rhythmic spasms in Tommy's constricted windpipe. He felt them weaken.

The back of his head was in the urinal, water trickled into his hair. His nose tingled with the smell of cake disinfectant. A blue smell. It brought him around. He let Tommy go and rolled out from under him. Tommy got to his knees and rubbed his Adam's apple and gasped for breath.

"Crazy mother," he gagged.

Fran stood by the sinks. The tears ran down his face. Tommy looked away.

They cleaned up without saying another word. Tommy left first. Fran stayed until he had himself under control, then he went looking for Ray. He found him at his desk reading the morning paper and smoking a cigarette. Ray had given up cigarettes twice since Fran had known him. About three months.

"I just had it out with Tommy."

"You two mix it up?" Ray said, looking at Fran's wet hair.

"He told me you fired him."

"That's one of the reasons I wanted to see you early."

"He blames me."

"You are to blame. You work harder and write better. Somebody comes along works harder and writes better than you, so long to you, too, Scoop. Gotta be fair."

"You mean impartial, Ray. There's a difference."

Ray sucked on the cigarette and hacked out a laugh. "Better thicken up that skin if you want to be an editor."

"Who said I did?"

"Wise up to yourself." He thwacked his newspaper. "Look how you've brought Angela along. She did crackerjack for you on the death of this lady professor. Keep her at it. She's yours; use her."

A dusky, glistening Angela, naked and in chains — his to use as he pleased — rose up before his eyes. He lost the thread of what Ray was saying. Something about the assignment he had taken from Tommy.

The real Angela, decently clothed and unfettered, was busy at her cubbyhole desk in the morgue. She had already found the rolls of film from the 1924 paper and had placed them by the viewer. He fed the first roll through and scanned the headlines, taking careful note of the weather that long-ago winter. A hunch.

The lead story for Tuesday morning, January 29, concerned the congressional resolution for the resignation of Secretary of the

Navy Edwin Denby over his role in the Tea Pot Dome scandal. There was also a report about the arctic freeze that gripped the seacoast region through the weekend, culmininating Monday when temperatures did not rise above minus 12 all day. He moved on. Like the hunter who stares at a deer motionless in a thicket and sees only branches and twigs but, becoming aware of the deer, sees it to the exclusion of all else, he found the following item on page three.

STEEL HARBOR MAN FROZEN TO DEATH
(Special to the *Riverston Republic*)

STEEL HARBOR, Jan. 28 — The body of Donald P. Collins, 41, of Steel Harbor was recovered this morning from Brave Boat Island by search party. Collins, a commercial fisherman, had been missing since late Saturday when he failed to return from the Channel Islands estuary where he moored his dory.

Dr. Harold Tagen of Steel Harbor who examined the body stated that death had occurred sometime Saturday night. Cause of death was given as heart failure due to shock and exposure.

Justice of the Peace William "Bill" Wentworth who led the search party reported that the remains had been scavenged by an animal or animals unknown. Long-time residents of the community recalled a similar occurrence during the latter days of the Civil War. At that time feral dogs were blamed for the deaths of two local youths and a number of strays were exterminated. No such action is currently planned, Wentworth said.

The detail that struck him, like the familiar, always-the-same brown eyes of the deer in the thicket, was the name Tagen.

He asked Angela if they had the oldest papers, the ones back to 1863 when the *Republic* was founded. She hunted them down and he threaded the roll covering the winter of 1865 into the machine. The format of the old papers made tracing the story difficult. It took a long time just getting through January, and even then he wasn't sure the story hadn't slipped past. Headlines were nonexistent or organized under categories such as "Telegraphic Dispatches" or "Minutes of the City Council." Advertisements appeared in boldface on the front page. There was no weather news, but toward the end of the month he started running across stories that implied bad weather — tenement fires, a horse-trolley derailment, an increase in the mortality of the elderly. On the front page of the number for February 2, sandwiched between an account of Sherman's forces forty miles from Charleston and a two-column ad for "Fancy Goods & Fine Gold Watches," he came across the following item under "Notice of the County Sheriff."

> The needless deaths of two Steel Harbor lads at Wolf Neck this week caused complaint to this office concerning the peril posed by unchecked curs. This is to give notice that pursuant to the Ordinance on "Injurious Practices," Section 16, all stray animals will be impounded. Dog owners are advised to restrain their charges.

There followed a reprint of the ordinance governing the disposal of destructive animals, and that was it. He found nothing more, not even the boys' obituary notices. He had reached a bottleneck.

Wolf Neck.

He looked up and dialed Dr. Tagen's number. A woman answered. He asked to speak to the doctor. "Minute," she said. A long minute.

"Tagen."

Fran identified himself.

"Yes?" said the doctor, as if he had been expecting the call.

Fran told him about the 1924 newspaper account. "You were cited as the examining physician."

"Good God." He hadn't expected that.

Fran said that what struck him about the story was the similarity to recent events.

"That was a long time ago."

Fran asked if he recalled the case.

"I do."

"Do you recall other cases?"

"Not in my lifetime."

That sounded like an equivocation. "Are you familiar with the 1865 incident when two boys died?"

"I don't know any more about that than you do."

But he knew, that was the point. "History's your hobby. You may have come across other incidents."

"There are no other incidents."

Which meant he had looked. "What does Wolf Neck mean to you?"

"Just a name. Long out of use."

Fran said Woody Parker had used it to refer to the islands, and Wilma Swanson believed wolves once lived there and maybe still did. She had found a skull.

"A skull?"

"A wolf's," Fran said. "So what about the name?"

"I should think you'd know something about that yourself."

Fran didn't know what he was talking about.

"You're a Havenport Thomas, aren't you?"

"My grandparents were."

"No, I suppose you don't know. History is so much dust and mildew to your generation."

He was turning crotchety. Equivocation in disguise? Fran asked again. Where had the name Wolf Neck come from?

"I have more important things to tend to than school you in matters you should already know. It's a matter of public record. Look it up." He was panting.

"Where?"

"The old *Coastal Gazette.*"

"When?"

"The year Maine became a state. Now if you'll excuse me, I have a patient." He hung up.

Fran turned to Angela and found her watching him. She had

been listening and her eyes were shining, eager. He asked if she had heard of the *Gazette*. She said she hadn't but was sure the state library in Augusta had. He asked if she would like to do some research for him over there.

"I'm at your command."

She was kidding, but in her light laughter he heard the tinkling of chains.

18

THE medical examiner's office was located in the old wing of the county hospital. It was a dismal basement office adjacent to the morgue, with dank cinder-block walls lacquered in lime-green paint thick as frosting. The receptionist, a martially erect Negro woman in a starched white uniform, told Fran to wait. He turned to take a chair and recognized two reporters from Steel Harbor the day before. They were waiting, too.

One was from the Bangor paper, a winded, chain-smoking old war-horse, a Ray Neville who never made it off the street. The other was a stringer out of Boston, a young Seven-Sisters type in duffle coat, school scarf, and austerely clean hair. Conversation was strained once they learned who Fran was. This was his territory.

The first time Dr. Brower came through the swinging door he didn't stay long. He wore a green smock and carried a clipboard and as he picked up the receptionist's phone to make a call he saw the reporters closing in. "Mrs. Frost," he croaked, and fled back into the morgue.

"You'll have to wait," said Mrs. Frost.

Ten minutes later he was back with notes prepared.

"Questions?"

Cause of death in the Swanson case.

"Cerebrovascular accident." It was amazing what Brower did with those words — like a bullfrog on a summer night.

A stroke?

But hadn't she been decapitated?

"Absence of the enzyme, nonspecific esterase, in tissue sample taken from the decedent indicates the wounds were sustained shortly after death."

Not shortly before?

He reminded them of the cause of death, a massive hemorrhage in the right parietal lobe. "Such an insult could be sustained only from pathologically high blood pressure. A significant loss of blood before death would preclude such an event. Decapitation came afterwards."

How long after?

"Not long. The blood had to be near body temperature to flow so freely."

Was there a history of high blood pressure?

"You miss the point. The point is epinephrine-induced hypertension."

Epi . . . ?

"Adrenaline."

In other words, something scared her to death in the act of killing her.

"I hadn't thought of it in exactly those words."

What about the wounds?

"Clean. Not a trace of metal, rust, hair, saliva. All we can go on is what they look like. They look like animal bites."

Was there going to be an inquest?

"I am recommending such."

Was murder a possibility?

"That will be decided at the hearing."

Was there a link with the Comstock death?

"Let me say by way of an answer that we have petitioned for an order of exhumation."

Was Woody Parker a suspect?

"There are no suspects at this time."

Had Parker been released?

Brower took off his glasses and his eyes shrank. He wiped the lenses, put them back on, and his eyes bulged.

"Parker's out of jail. That's what that phone call was all about, wasn't it, Doc?" the Bangor reporter said. He flicked the stub of cigarette from his mouth and in the act of stomping on it wheeled and tramped out with Fran and the stringer on his heels. Mrs. Frost did not ask them to wait.

Their destination was the county courthouse. Fran knew a

shortcut and got there first. The Bangor reporter was next in a beat-up Dodge and the stringer last in her beige Honda. They scuffed up gritty granite steps through the revolving door into the lobby where the marble floor echoed their footsteps with a busy zing. Fran led the way down a corridor of tall, open doorways. Toward the back of the building the tall doors were closed. Bars appeared. The smell was of wet wool, the close, indoors winter smell you feel you're catching pneumonia in.

Fran recognized the yellow-faced lawyer in the camel-hair coat. He was talking to a bailiff. Woody came into view fastening his belt. Caroline held his coat and hat. She had on a dressy wool skirt, hose, and high heels. Fran admired her legs.

She tensed when she saw him. She saw the others, too, and tried to protect her uncle from them, but from him she tried to protect herself. The others asked questions but he held back. Part of this was strategy. To have asked certain questions risked giving away what he knew exclusively. The other part was her. Each time he came in contact with her he felt the shock of her presence. She was the only thing real to him, the only thing that mattered. He felt that if he reached out and touched her they would melt into one another, bond, at the point of contact. So the others asked questions and he hung back. And she shielded her uncle from them and herself from him. But every so often her eyes sought him out, longing for him and dreading his coming.

With Woody between them, Caroline and the lawyer made a dash down the corridor to the lobby and through the revolving door where Woody got squeezed between the panels and made a complete rotation back into the arms of the reporters. Fran handed him along and he tumbled out to his niece. The door discharged them one at a time, like rounds from a pistol, down the steps to the lawyer's car. Fran held the passenger-side door for Caroline and out of the others' hearing asked if he could see her the next day.

Her whispered *yes* raised the hair on the back of his neck.

The car drove away. He walked across the street to the VW. The broad back of the Bangor reporter shambled ahead of him toward the Happy Hour Club on the other side of the railroad tracks. There was a phone there and dingy, quiet booths.

"Fran?" The stringer stood in the open door of her Honda. "Are you having an affair with that woman?" She smiled chummily. "You can tell me to go to hell."

He did.

"Ah," she said, wrinkling her bobbed, perfect little nose. "In that case be careful. There's something weird about that one. Witchy."

He went back to the office. On the way upstairs he ran into Tommy Blackburn. Tommy and his buddy the ad accounts manager were talking by the stairwell window. They darted looks as he passed. He didn't have time to worry about it. He had a page-one story budgeted, of which he had yet to write a word, with less than an hour to deadline. He stepped inside the newsroom and Ray flew at him like a bat. He sat down to work and tried to ignore Ray hovering over his shoulder. After the lead and into the second paragraph Ray showed his approval by going away and bothering somebody else.

It all worked out. It always did. Fran met his deadline — barely — and the copy editor met his — barely — and so on down the line. Night was suddenly outside the windows, a *fait accompli*. The newsroom began to empty. Fran found Angela's note as he was putting his desk in order. She had called to say that she found the story, but the microfilm photostated poorly and she had to write much of it out longhand. The roads were bad and she would be late. She had a surprise for him.

Ray stopped by on his way out. "Working late?"

Fran said he was waiting for Angela.

"Well, I hope you two get out of here at a decent hour. It's easy to lose perspective." Now that tomorrow's edition was tucked in safe and sound, Hyde had become Jekyll. He dug a cigarette out of the pack in his breast pocket, reconsidered, put it back.

"Wedding anniversary tomorrow. Need a special kind of place. You know what I mean — candles, wine, seafood, moonlight on the bay — not a tourist trap."

Fran thought of suggesting the Widow's Walk Inn, but in winter that would have been a little stark. Generally when somebody said he didn't want a tourist trap it meant he did want one, but not a cheap one. "Try Camden," he said. "Camden has lots of places like that."

"Will do. Peg's forever trying to get me to eat those big red spiders."

"How many years, Ray?"

"Twenty-three . . . or is it four."

"To what do you attribute your marital success? Our readers are eager to hear."

Ray's eyes narrowed. He thought Fran was making fun of him. "You really want to know?"

"With my track record it might be a good idea."

"Most people don't."

"I do."

"I doubt that. You're still looking for happiness." He turned up the collar of his overcoat. "Night, Scoop."

Fran heard the squeak of Ray's rubbers (who but Ray still wore shoe rubbers?) on the stairs, then the louder squeak of the door. He felt the rumble of the presses starting up below. The overhead lights jiggled so that the air itself seemed to vibrate. Every second light had been turned off and made the newsroom a shadowy checkerboard. The downstairs door squeaked again and he felt a draft. There was scuttling on the stairs and then Angela bobbed through the doorway.

"Got it," she said, clacking across the newsroom, her aluminum cane glinting in and out of light and shadow. She tossed a manila folder on his desk. He flipped through the several pages of photocopy. Much of the negative image, cramped white lettering on black background was illegible, but Angela had written out the rough parts in her perfect hand.

"What's the surprise?"

"Read it."

The Coastal Weekly Gazette, Friday, February 11, 1820.
(Published every Friday morning)

INTERESTING MISCELLANY

In the following communication, we recognize the considerable lights of one whose correspondence is not unknown to these pages, nor, we venture, unfamiliar to the eye of an habitual reader.

Sir — Having been privileged to observe the brave undertaking by the citizens of Steele Harbour with regard to the extermination of a verminous infestation of Wolves from that community, Your Correspondent is pleased to impart the details of those events which transpired Friday and Saturday last. Such an endeavor was necessitated by the recent prodigious loss of livestock; to wit, some three of cattle, two each of oxen and swine, and at least one dog, a house pet. Although husbandmen of the region have suffered losses in the past through the agency of foraging Wolves, those raids were sporadic and did not constitute a sustained campaign. This unnaturally frosty Winter has emboldened the predators with hunger to the extent that they have become not just a Nuisance but a Menace.

The scheme to entrap the miscreants was communicated to Your Correspondent by Major Francis Thomas, U.S. Army, Ret., of nearby Havenport on Wednesday the Second of the month, and an invitation to observe was extended. Fresh signs of activity from the Pack were detected that very Friday in the vicinity known as the Channel Islands, a broad waste of unproductive marsh and island wood situated north of town on Penobscot Bay. An Ox unfit for labour on account of extreme age was transported to the site and tethered by rope from a gambrel iron piercing the hock to a stake driven into the frost. This method of impedance was hoped to attract the Wolves both by the smell of blood and the lamentations of the unhappy creature. Members of the shooting party, a hundred strong, composed of volunteers from as far away as Riverston, retired to the wood and waited in ambuscade with various firearms.

The wait was long, the conditions severe; no fire which might Warm the men but Warn the quarry was permitted; no conversation which might lighten a hundred hearts was allowed. We waited past dark, beset by conditions of such inclemency that doubts were voiced as to the efficacy of powder and ball.

Past midnight (Your Correspondent cannot be more exact owing to the circumstance, that, no doubt due to the extreme cold, his timepiece stopped at a quarter past the hour), an inhuman call was heard across the wastes, followed thereon by others in diverse pitch. The Ox, which in exhaustion had ceased complaint and collapsed on the crusty snow, laboured to its feet and snorted. From the dark of the wood we could see across the moonlit plain and observe those shadowy forms, some eight or nine in number, approach eagerly from the North. The Ox was thrown into a frenzy and pawed the snow with such wild fright its wound bled afresh.

The Wolves, brutes with luxuriant Winter pelts and ravening maws, circled the doomed beast and pressed the attack. The valiant Ox lowered its horns to defend itself. One bold Wolf pranced close to lap the blood from the snow, never taking its eyes from the formidable horns. In vain the Ox charged as its adversary skirted the reach of the tether. A ripping sound was heard accompanied by a bellow of pain as the gambrel drew taut. The Wolf applied its jaws to the bovine snout and held firm even as it was raised entirely off its feet as the Great Ox turned and charged the woods, intending, it must be assumed, to smash its tormentor into the nearest tree. This time the gambrel tore cleanly through the hamstring tendon and the splendid beast crashed to the ice, crushing the Wolf beneath him. The Ox did not rise again. The Pack was on him in an instant and commenced feeding before the hapless animal was entirely dead.

There arose a murmur of outrage from the men, but Major Thomas passed the word that no action was to be taken until the

Wolves had had their fill, as he wanted them Meat Drunk. The assemblage waited in disciplined order whilst that other wild assembly partook of the steaming cadaver, which was reduced to scraps of hide and bone in a matter of minutes. The Gluttony of the feasters, combined with the uncouth noise of the repast, excited the men to the limits of restraint until that awful moment when the Major commissioned the bugle to be blown. Our battle cry broke the silence of the night; torches were lit, firearms discharged, and the long line of men moved forward from the wood.

The Pack was confounded, some individuals taking flight, others running in circles and turning on their own kind. One attempted to infiltrate the line directly and was shot dead by a fusillade from that sector. The survivors withdrew to the outer reaches of the marsh where their flight was interrupted by the Bay. Most would have perished on the spot, yet a few might have broken through to wreak havoc another day, but for a curious phenomenon of Nature. An Ice Bridge communicating with the island chain had formed across the narrows, and rather than turn on their persecutors whilst darkness was to their advantage, the Wolves bounded across the icy isthmus and so sealed their fate. Major Thomas commanded that a watch fire be built at the point of access and maintained throughout the night. The order was carried out immediately and the result was that no Wolf crossed back to the mainland through the remaining hours of darkness, although terrible howls were heard, and on more than one occasion the gleam of eyes, reflecting the glow of the great fire, was observed at the edge of the island wood.

At first light the Major led his men across the Ice Bridge and organized a Phalanx. Word of the party's success had spread overnight and the ranks were doubled. Various breeds of hunting dog were pressed into service, and their urgent baying rang out in the crisp dawn air. As the formation set out, the Major left instructions that the watch fire be maintained by the rear pickets so no Wolf might double back and escape.

The Channel Islands are some five in number, the five becoming one at low tide, connected by a bar of mud flat, eel grass, and shingle. Two are but insignificant granite promontories, the remainder are wooded, and the second of these of appreciable size.

The Wolves took refuge in the interior of the large island where they were found out and destroyed. By afternoon the tally stood at seven. The pelts were taken as proof of kill for bounty, a not inconsiderable sum of Twenty Dollars per animal levied by Massachusetts Statute.

With the approach of dusk most of the volunteers departed in anticipation of the Sabbath, but Major Thomas remained unappeased by the day's showing and organized one last foray before nightfall. Concern was voiced that the remaining Wolf, or Wolves (the exact number not having been fixed), might avoid observation by so depleted a rank, and the Phalanx was discarded in favor of hunting parties. The Major's party, some ten strong, including Your Correspondent, proceeded to an icy bog of coniferous growth on the landwards shore of the big island, where, at a distance of some hundred yards, a Wolf of impressive size was observed near the skinned corpse of another killed earlier in the day. The animal appeared harried and oppressed, of matted pelt and slouched posture, the suspicious snout dividing its time equally between the carrion and the air. Fortunately, the party's scent did not carry in the becalmed twilight, and our aspect was obscured by tall trees to the rear.

Major Thomas rejected a suggestion to move closer for a better shot, proposing instead that we fire in volley so as to increase our chance of a hit. Accordingly, each man took aim, hung fire, and discharged on command. The shock of the report was deafening. A cloud of smoke hid the target from view, then lifted like a curtain to reveal the unhappy monster prostrate and writhing on the ice. We approached and observed the Wolf furiously biting its wounded flank. Crimson blood bubbled in a singular fashion from the mouth, an indication, according to the Major, of a lung shot. As the all too human eyes surveyed each man in turn, the Major sprang forward and decapitated the animal with his sabre. The skinned corpse from the morning's hunt was found to have been a female, prompting speculation that the current kill, a male, had been its mate.

A ninth Wolf was not discovered, although at the Major's behest the hunt continued past darkness. Your Correspondent conjectured that the distortions of moonlight and shadow had misrepresented the number, and that all the Wolves were in fact accounted for, an opinion readily subscribed to by most of those present. As no domestic animal has been molested nor predator observed these several days since, the action must be regarded as an unqualified success.

Pronaque cum spectant Animalia caetera Terram,
Os Homini sublime dedid, Coelumque tueri Jussit . . .

Ovid, *Metamorphoses*

Fran was aware again of the rumble of the presses, the tremor of the lights, Angela sitting on his desk and looking down at him, her eyes positively owlish.

"Are you related to that old guy?"

"I think so."

No wonder he had felt so close to the story. There must have been clues, things he knew without knowing he knew, long forgotten incidents from childhood, anecdotes and attitudes, a family legacy as real as an inherited nose or mannerism.

"Know what I think?" Angela said. "I think the major was right. There must have been a ninth wolf, a pregnant female." She shivered, but not at all uncomfortably. She had caught his excitement. "They've been there all these years. Hiding. Inbred and horrible. You know, deformed."

Her cane clattered to the floor and spooked them both.

She sat facing him with her stockinged knees pressed together, her calves dangling at his side. He put the pages back into the folder and stood up. "There's no more proof of that than there is for coyotes or dogs or a madman," he said. His voice was cool, almost censorious.

He picked up her cane and handed it to her. There was a question in her eyes that his refused to answer.

They left the building together and he walked her to her car. The night was shivery cold, with dampness creeping up from the river. He started to put his arm around her and then didn't. Her rusty Toyota was parked next to his VW, bumpers almost touching.

"What'cha doing for dinner?" she said.

He didn't know what to say.

"Want to come over to my place?" Her hot breath exploded in steam under the streetlight. "I make pizza from scratch. We could pick up some beer at Jimmy's on the way."

Jimmy's was not on the way to Angela's, but she knew that the old-fashioned market was part of Fran's world. It was her way of acknowledging his world and offering to accommodate her own with his. Her invitation extended far beyond the sharing of a pizza, made from scratch.

He imagined saying yes. He imagined her apartment, although he had never been inside; the warmth, the smell of dough and oregano, candlelight perhaps — sort of an Italian restaurant with a bed in the back. What a treasure she would be. What a gift. But he couldn't accept it. He could not because he did not love her. That wouldn't matter with a lot of women, but with this one it did. He had to work with her every day. Ray had practically made him her supervisor. But most of all, professional considerations aside, it was because she was poised to fall in love. She was at the edge of a cliff and all she needed was a little push.

He stepped back. "No thanks, Angie." He had intended to say more, to make an excuse, to let her down easy, but when it came to love there was no way of letting someone down easy. It always hurt.

Before he could do anything about it she put her arms under his and hugged him close, pushing her nose into the softness of his fleece collar. His own arms dangled above, afraid they would touch her, touch her hair or waist, and not be able to stop. Then just as suddenly as she had embraced him she let go and ran to her car. She got in, started the engine, revved it until the wizened valves shrieked, and drove away. To go home she had to make a U-turn and come back by him. When she did he saw that she had caught the hem of her coat in the car door and that a piece of it was flapping. He had been doing pretty well until then, but the sight of that little flag of flight and defeat broke him.

As he turned towards his own car he caught the movement of a figure stepping back into the shadows out of range of the street-light. The person seemed to have been in a dark cloak of some kind and moved very — even unnaturally — fast. But then again it was hard to be sure of anything because of his burning eyes.

19

WHEN Fran went down to his car in the morning he found long, claw-like scratches slashed across the hood. They raked in a swath from the windshield wiper on the driver's side to the headlamp, and were deep enough to gouge the metal as well as peel the paint.

"Something wrong, Mr. Thomas?" Jimmy was opening up across the street.

Vandals, Fran said, and Jimmy ambled over. He had earmuffs on and a greasy down vest over his apron. Feathers stuck out of the vest like an old pillow.

"Looks like bear, don't it?"

"More like one of those garden claws," Fran said. He was glad to have somebody to talk to.

"All those I ever seen's had three prongs. This here has five." He checked the cars parked in front and behind Fran's. "None of the rest's been vandalized. Made yourself a enemy, could be."

Fran thought of the cloaked figure stepping back from the light. Had he been followed home last night? He asked Jimmy to keep an eye out. Probably nothing to it, he said. Reporters made enemies all the time and had to take it in stride. He was shaking. If Jimmy noticed he didn't let on.

On the way to Steel Harbor he passed the paper mill. With dock butting the river ice and smokestacks puffing above a super-structure traversed by frosty catwalks, it looked like a great ice-bound ship. Clouds of white steam trailed south in the sluggish Canadian currents that descended with glacial persistence from Hudson Bay. When the smoke changed direction the weather would break. All his years in the Sunbelt he had craved the change of seasons that brought cold weather, forgetting the force the cold could be. It was there to greet you when you got out of bed in the morning, and keep you company when you climbed back in at night. It sought out your weaknesses like a patient enemy and whispered to your bones of death. It wore you down, physically and mentally, and long bouts of it could break you.

Past the mill he saw Ed Hentov's Blazer coming the other way. Ed was alone, freshly shaven and pale, on his way to work. He didn't see Fran and Fran didn't honk.

His first stop in Steel Harbor was Dr. Tagen's. He knocked at the front and heard the ticking of heavy paws and loud, investigative sniffs. Then footsteps, not the slow strides of an old man but the quick little steps of an old woman. The door opened.

"Not sick are you?" said a stump of a person in her seventies, red in the face and wide as the door.

Fran said he wasn't sick.

"That's fortunate, because the doctor's not feeling so chipper today himself." At her sides where there were slight indications of a waist the two Great Danes peeped out. "Took to bed yesterday. Got all fluttery." She threw a hip into the dog trying to squeeze past on her right.

Fran asked if she might be Mrs. Tagen. The woman found this desperately funny.

"I'm housekeeper and nothing but," she said, winking a roguish, puffy eye. "Though lord knows there's more than one woman that calls herself a housekeeper and does a sight more in the bedroom than tidy up."

There was movement on the landing above. "Mimi, who's there?"

Fran called up his name.

"Ask him up, Mimi."

The old stairway was the most solid wooden one Fran had ever climbed. Not a creak, and he felt the hardness of each step through his boots. Dr. Tagen waited at the top in a whipcord robe and slippers, his skin as milky as white quartz.

"I'd shake hands but you've brought in the cold." The doctor stepped back through double doors into a low bedchamber. An easy chair and a deacon's bench faced one another in the space between the four-poster and the mantle of the plastered-over fireplace. He eased into the chair and fussily arranged the comforter across his kness. Fran took the bench. It was hard and too close to the doctor. He could smell the old man's smell.

For starters Fran said that he had read the account of the wolf hunt.

"Tell me," said blue lips stretched across teeth as yellow and shrunken as seed corn, "how directly are you related to your namesake, Major Francis Thomas?"

Fran said the major was not his namesake. He was named after his mother's father, whose name had been Frank. His father's father, Grampy Thomas, never talked about the major. Fran had been full of questions, too, as a boy, because the major's grave was on the farm.

Dr. Tagen said that sounded right. Fran was almost surely a direct descendant on the Thomas side. It sounded right, too, that his grandfather had avoided the subject.

Why was that?

"Because the major hanged himself. He hanged himself out there on the islands the winter following the hunt."

The room was hot and drafty at the same time. Heat rose in waves from the floor register. The ancient horsehair plaster smelled like stagnant water.

"Did you know you were related to the Parkers here in town?" the doctor went on.

"Woody Parker?" Fran almost said Caroline.

The major was survived by two children, a son and daughter. The son married before the old man's death, the daughter stayed home as the woman of the house after the early death of her mother. The major's death freed her. She married a Steel Harbor Parker. Dr. Tagen knew all this because Aston Parker, Woody's father, took an interest in the family tree after the boy began acting strangely. Aston was afraid that insanity ran in the family because of the major's suicide.

"So Woody's my uncle?"

Five times removed, the doctor figured. But that wasn't the important thing. The important thing was that the major's blood flowed through his veins, and like Woody he was susceptible to the influence of the islands.

"What influence?"

"I don't know." Dr. Tagen didn't look like he'd seen a ghost — he looked like he was one. "All I can tell you is that it's as intangible as a shadow. And as tenacious."

Fran's palms grew clammy. His stomach pressed against his racing heart.

"Those boys who died," the doctor went on, "the ones you asked about over the phone. One was a Parker and the other a Thomas. They were cousins."

He felt a rush of air. Falling. Kicking. Hauled up short. A sunburst of death.

The vertigo passed in an instant, or so it seemed, but when he came to himself he saw that a horrible change had come over the doctor's face. The mouth was a great round O. He heard a moan. It took a moment to connect the noise with that cave of a mouth. He rose to help just as the Great Danes burst through the double doors, their hysterical barking in that low room amplified to bright and dancing pain. He was driven back to the bench. The black dog set itself between its master and him and worked itself into a frenzy. He did not move. He did not look into the animal's eyes. The spotted dog slipped behind him between the bench and the window. He caught a glimpse of its pacing shadow on the wall.

The doctor's moan had gradually become the housekeeper's name. "Mimi," he cried. "Mimi."

She bustled in on stubby legs and threatened the dogs with a potent churn of the hips. "Lys! Skygge! Get away, you cussed beasts."

She lifted the doctor under the arms. "Give us a hand," she said to Fran in the same tone of voice she used with the dogs.

The husk of a body was surprisingly light but awkward to carry, a bundle of sticks. They laid him on the bed. The housekeeper asked if she should fetch Alby Sergeant and he shook his head, no. She propped up the pillows and he took a sip of water and wetted his lips. They were scaly and blood oozed between the cracks because the mouth had been stretched so wide. He looked at Fran.

"Susceptibility. That's a medical term. *The fathers have eaten sour grapes, and the children's teeth are set on edge.* That's the Bible." The eyes rolled over to the housekeeper without the head moving. "I'll rest now."

The housekeeper saw Fran downstairs. The dogs followed, calm now, as if nothing had happened. The black dog even gave him a nudge in the seat of the pants as he was putting on his jacket.

"Skygge's trying to make up," the woman said.

"And the other one's Lys," Fran said. "What kind of names are those?"

"Danish, I suppose. The doctor's people come from over there, you know. The peculiar part of it is, for as long as I've known him — and that goes back some — he's owned a pair of big galoots like these and always with the same names."

She told him this as she opened the door to the street. He was surprised when she stepped outside with him. She crossed her meaty arms and slapped them to keep warm.

"What set him off?" she said in a lowered voice. "Goodness knows it don't take much."

Fran said he didn't know.

"What was that noise, then? Heard it plain as day through the register."

"You mean his moaning?"

"No, before that. Sounded like a snap. Like when you twist the head off a trout."

20

HE caught Mrs. Parker alone in the coffee shop during the lull between the last wave of breakfasts and the first wave of coffee breaks. When she saw him coming she set to scouring the counter as if she had an old score to settle with toast crumbs and coffee rings. He told her he wanted to see Caroline.

"Thought as much," she said without looking up.

"She around?"

"I never know where she is anymore."

Her face remained bent to the task. He glanced down at the wet counter top and their eyes met in its sheen.

"Door at the end of the lobby. She'll be up by now."

He thanked her and started away.

"Make sure your boots are clean. I have a Persian rug in that hall."

He knocked at the door at the end of the lobby. His boots were clean. He had wiped them on the Persian rug. The door opened a crack and the steamy, intimately feminine atmosphere of a scented bath puffed out at him. A wet hand crept out around the edge, then a wet, hot face appeared.

"Um, hello," Caroline said. She asked him in.

She was wrapped in a housecoat of soft blue quilting, her throat bare and hair twisted and dripping. She gave off the dewy aura of hyacinth and disturbed him so much that he had to look away. He saw a bedroom with mussed sheets on the unmade bed. He averted his eyes and found himself looking into a bathroom where a pair of woman's slippers lay beside the sweating ball-and-claw-foot tub. He blushed like a girl. Caroline blushed like a girl, too.

He waited in the parlor while she dressed. He heard the whir of her hair dryer behind the bedroom door. The parlor was the center of the small apartment she shared with her mother. There were a braided rug, two wing chairs and an ottoman, a fireplace with French-white moldings. A framed photograph on the mantle caught his attention, a studio enlargement of a snapshot, touched up in the unnatural color of its day. A young family man no older than himself held the hand of a little girl. On the other side of the child stood a younger, happier Mrs. Parker. It looked like Easter Sunday. Mother and daughter wore hats and white gloves. A raw, early Easter, judging by the tails of the father's topcoat flapping in the wind. Little Caroline, whose hair in the picture was tinted the flagrant red of an autumn maple leaf, had been caught in the doleful expression that turns children into ageless trolls. He saw how tightly she clutched her father's hand and how she and her mother didn't touch at all.

The dryer stopped and the bedroom door swung open. He heard the staticky pull of a brush through hair. "I suppose you want me to take you to Uncle Woody," she said, hidden from view.

He told her about the 1924 newspaper story that Woody had given him a lead on. He said he wondered if Woody had seen something back then that influenced the way he was today.

"I have something to show you." Her voice was breathless, as if she were bending over as she spoke. He heard the rub of cloth against skin and the pull of a zipper. She came out of the bedroom in a soft gray sweater and white jeans. Her clean hair swayed with the movement of her body. In her arms was a dirty, tattered leather-bound photo album.

"This was my grandmother's. The police found it at Uncle Woody's."

They sat across from one another in the wing chairs and she opened the album on the ottoman. She turned the stiff, black pages pasted with old snapshots and keepsakes to the middle and took out a sheaf of papers. There were sheets of stationery, envelopes, pieces of construction paper, bits of brown paperbag, some old and brittle, some new, and on each was a crude but detailed drawing of a wolf. Not the same wolf. Some were females with rows of saw-toothed dugs; others had jaws agape with weird, malformed fangs. One shrewd fellow had the closed, zipper mouth, the tall ears and long snout of Anubis, the Egyptian jackal god of the dead. The style as much as anything made Fran think of ancient Egypt. Each was rigid in profile, immobily stylized and repetitious, as if the soul were imprisoned in a form it was doomed to wear forever — immortality as a curse rather than a blessing.

"Do you think these are what he saw?" she said.

"I think they're what he thought he saw."

He asked if he could borrow a few. He promised not to show them to anyone or put them in the newspaper without her permission. She consented.

They took his car to Woody's. In the turnout they found a pickup truck with a rifle rack across the rear window and an NRA bumper sticker. Caroline was afraid the bullies hadn't done with her uncle, but Fran said his story on the medical examiner's report had probably brought out the hunters. Not long afterwards they heard the distant double crack — the shot and its echo — of a rifle fired down in the flats.

He knew the camp was empty long before they got there. There was no chimney smoke. Closer in he saw that the door was padlocked. But most of all there was no tingle down the spine to tell him they were being watched.

"He's hiding out," Caroline said. "He won't be back until everybody's gone."

Woody was in no danger of being tracked. The meadow had been trampled by snowmobiles and men on foot. Caroline dug a pull-tab out of the snow and plinked it into the empty root beer can she picked up next to it.

"Why are you men so destructive?"

"Hey, I'm not destructive," Fran said.

She looked at him skeptically. She was suddenly the scowling troll he had seen in the photograph on the mantle.

They walked back to the car. It was parked with the front end to the snowbank so that when they came over the top Caroline couldn't help but notice the scratches on the hood. She stopped and looked down, and since he had already descended the bank he had to turn and look up at her. He knew right away what she was staring at.

"My friend Jimmy thinks I've made an enemy," he said.

"You have?" The thing that chilled him about her answer, apart from the complete lack of sympathy in her voice, was that it seemed as much a statement of fact as a question.

All the way to town her mood held. She was unapproachable in this state, eyes like clear, deep ice and lips puckered in the bud of a pout. Yet he was drawn to her all the more intensely. There was a dirty feel to it, as if he were a sort of child molester. She was right about men.

When they stopped in front of the inn he did not want to let her go. "Did you know we're related?" he said. She looked out the window up the steps but made no effort to get out of the car. "Dr. Tagen says the Parkers and Thomases are branches off the same family tree. We're fifth cousins."

"Kissing cousins." She turned and looked at him. The ice in her eyes had melted. "Isn't that what you mean, Fran?"

He felt a thrill of tenderness when she said his name.

"Say what you mean and we'll get along better."

"I mean to ask you out to dinner tonight."

21

HAZEL Wentworth saw him coming. She had a built-in early warning system against favor seekers. Always doing for others and where did it get her?

"I suppose your mother never taught you to close a door."

He was sorry. He had been thinking of someone — something — else. He went back and closed the door.

"Don't stand there wasting my time. What do you want?"

He wanted to look at the record of deeds.

"If I dropped dead tomorrow, then where would you all be?" She showed him the property file and map cabinets, both of oak, one slim and the other stout, like Jack Sprat and his wife. "Put everything back the way you found it. Oh, better let me. You'll only make a mess."

He was not put off. The house of secrets was often guarded by a witch. He opened the long drawer of the map cabinet and took out the heavy sheaf of maps and placed it on the lectern top. The Brave Boat Island region was the fortieth of forty detailed town maps. He found the boathouse lot on the southwest shore, a sizable piece of property longer than it was deep, shaped like an inverted California. The name Hentov had been penciled in over another. He could make out the smudge of the erasure. Armed with the map and lot numbers he looked up the property card. Duly entered was the record of title and a description of twenty acres of woodland with 1,600 feet of frontage and a boathouse, purchased in 1973 for $12,600.00 by Edward Nansen Hentov from Samuel Comstock.

As clearly as he could picture Caroline Parker's sea-green eyes, Fran saw the town drunk staggering across the ice that fierce calm night on his befuddled way to sleep it off in the boathouse he had once owned.

His years as a reporter in Southern California put him on the lookout for some kind of real estate power play. He went back to the map. There were several other lots on Brave Boat Island in private hands. He recognized the name Collins, the family of the dead fisherman having held on to the ancestral boatslip. The map showed that large tracts of the island were publicly owned, and there were no maps at all of the outer islands. He needed help.

Hazel?

"Do you know what time of year it is? It's the first of the year, for your information. Tax time. I'm up to here. I'm swamped. I can't be bothered." She got up from her desk and gave her skirt a tug. "Here's Mal Boulding. Pester him. I'm going to lunch." She put on a black coat trimmed with rodent fur and whisked out.

The chief had come in on her last words and held the door as she swept past. He strolled back to the files and studied the map on the lectern.

"Ed Hentov?"

Fran laid out his suspicions.

"How well do you know Ed?" Mal said after hearing him through.

"Not very."

"Can't say I do either, and we've both lived in this town all our lives. I know his character, though. A man can't hide that, and personal pride is what Ed Hentov is all about. I wouldn't put killing past him. He's capable. But he wouldn't be sneaky about it, and it wouldn't have a thing to do with money."

Even so, the chief helped track down Ed's other holdings and put through a call to Augusta. They found nothing to indicate that Ed or anybody else was interested in the Channel Islands. Fran was the first to give up. Mal kept at it, rummaging through the tax rolls after he'd finished with Hazel's binders of deeds and yellow sheets. He had a big man's momentum, slow to get started but impossible to stop once he was rolling.

"Judas Iscariot."

Hazel stood on the other side of the counter watching Mal

paw through her books. "I can't turn my back a minute. Not a minute."

They escaped to the chief's office. Fran was smiling. Mal sat down at his desk and took an oversized envelope from the top drawer and slid it across.

"These came back from the lab."

The smile on Fran's face flattened out like the line of an EKG when the patient dies.

The envelope contained three eight-by-ten black and white photographs, each showing a brightly lit nighttime landscape in sharp focus. In one the flash was reflected by sparkling disks on the snow. He couldn't make them out until he remembered Wilma's plan to use sardines as a lure. Another was a close-up of what looked like a brass eyelet on a tarpaulin. The third was a long-distance shot. He recognized the barkless trunk of the dead hemlock, bone white against the black woods. With the tree as a reckoning point he reconstructed the scene. Wilma had established her observation post on the icy neck between the islands. She had seeded the snow with bait and hidden in a blind with her back to the bay. He arranged the photographs in sequence, and taking into account the time it took to shoot, reset, and focus a manually operated 35-millimeter camera — the camera she had used that day in the barn to shoot the doe — he went through them again.

But what had she been shooting? Whatever it was, it didn't show up on film. Whatever it was, it was coming right at her. Suddenly, as in a primitive cartoon, he saw those crude stick figures of Woody's superimposed on the photographs and rushing across the neck.

22

THE taproom windows blazed orange. Above them the pale slab of wall loomed in the starlight against the pitch-black upper-story windows. What little moisture there was had frozen in midair and danced in the light of the downstairs windows. The snow underfoot was granular and no more slippery than sand. Its squeak set Fran's teeth on edge and caused the wool lining of his gloves to feel unbearably coarse against his fingertips. Yet he was warm enough, even feverish, as if the hearth of his heart fed on the cold, the dark, the stars, and the keenness of frost that was like the smell of stars.

Inside, the air was as dry and hot as the air outside was dry and cold. The tavern smells were overpowering, as were the bright lights. His boots on the hardwood floor sounded too loud, so did his knock on the door at the end of the hall.

Caroline's full, pale face, like the full moon, appeared before him. She showed none of her moony vagueness, though. Tonight her eyes were keen, focused as lasers, on the gray side of green, sidelong and expectant. As he helped her on with her coat he let his cheek brush her hair.

"Thank you," she said, giving him the sidelong eyes and full white face.

They took the Whiskey Springs road to Route 1. On the way they passed the sign to Havenport at the intersection of the Star Route, a dark, rolling, ancient little road that came by its name from following the north star.

"Our mutual ancestor lived out that way," he said as they turned onto broad, clear, well-lit Route 1. Caroline looked back.

"What's there?"

"The farm."

"You've been there?"

"I used to spend vacations there when my grandparents were alive."

"Have you been recently?"

"Not since my parents sold it."

"Where are they?"

"Connecticut."

She thought a bit. "You'll have to take me sometime."

Near the ferry landing on the Rockland waterfront they found the restaurant Caroline had in mind. It didn't look like much more than a diner outside, but inside the green, bubbling salt water of the lobster tank and the flickering candlelight gave the dining room a dreamy, underwater feel. The smell was of steamed seafood and lemon and hot butter.

"I wasn't going to order one of those because they weren't red," said a familiar voice. "Spiders are supposed to be red."

Fran turned to find Ray and Peg Neville regarding him from a nearby booth, a bottle of champagne between them. They hadn't been served yet, but Ray was wearing a lobster bib. Peg's hair was teased and sprayed up into a platinum helmet, her darker eyes lively above the taut mask of a recent face-lift. The drawn skin tugging at the corners of her mouth gave her a serene smile.

Fran introduced Caroline to them and had the out-of-body sensation of seeing her fresh through their eyes, as if she were a charming stranger. In the long coat that covered the tops of her high boots she looked like a beautiful Cossack.

Ray had an idea. Why didn't they join Peg and him in a toast to celebrate their anniversary? He ordered another bottle and glasses and he and Peg made room in the booth. The manager himself brought the champagne. Ray proposed a toast. The sparkle of the wine went directly from the glass into Caroline's eyes.

Peg was fascinated by her. "Hon," she said in her panhandle twang, "your skin is as soft as a baby's butt. Ray, just look at this skin."

"We got lost on the way to Camden and ended up here," Ray said to Fran. "Lucky break, huh?" There was a challenge in his irony. He knew about Peg and protected her.

Peg started telling Caroline about her interest in "the spiritual realm." She considered herself a "sensitive" and had attended seances and study groups in palmistry and the tarot deck. The next time Fran looked, she had captured Caroline's hand on the table and was showing her her life and love lines.

"Loyalty is your strong suit. This interferes with the expression of your deepest needs."

Caroline looked at Fran. Get me out of this, the look said. He hunted through his closet of excuses for one that fit.

Ray came to the rescue. "Hey there, Peg-o-my-heart, these kids want to be left alone." He leaned over and gave her a squeeze. "That goes for us kids, too."

Peg shrugged him off. She was so engrossed in the lines of Caroline's palm that she allowed her chin to sag into her neck. This caused the tucked skin around the jaw to double under in tight, reptilian creases. Fran wondered why somebody so full of life would take such pains to deaden her appearance. Because that's what it amounted to. The death mask that surgery had made of her lower face, the powder and blush applied with the heavy hand of a mortician, the metallic hair and matching eye shadow and nails comprised a sort of living sarcophagus.

Caroline freed her hand and hid it under the table. "Please," she said, fixing those high-voltage eyes on Peg's. They were a color Fran hadn't seen them before. Violet.

The sarcophagus swung open. Inside was an old woman buried alive — a wrinkled, grimacing, agonizing crone. The vision passed swiftly, like a hallucination that is there out of the corner of the eye but not there when the eye turns full. The lines had set in her make-up, though, making her look permanently aged. Seeing the others' faces she took out her compact and looked at herself in the mirror.

"Shoot." She pushed Ray to let her get out of the booth.

Caroline asked if she could help.

"No." There was fear in Peg's voice. Then more calmly, "No, Hon, I'll be all right. It was all that bubbly."

"She never could hold her liquor," Ray said. He was ashen.

When Peg came back from the powder room, her face restored to lifelessness, Fran and Caroline wished the Nevilles a happy anniversary and left the restaurant. Out on Route 1 they stopped at Moody's, a truck stop that looked like a diner outside and was a diner inside. They ordered hamburgers.

"What happened back there?"

"Who knows," Caroline said. Her face was troubled.

"I can ask Ray about it tomorrow."

She took his hand in hers. "I'd rather you didn't."

He looked down at the long hand and unpolished nails. He turned it over and examined the palm under the diner's fluorescent glare. The lines looked normal to him. He put his own palm next to hers. Yes, perfectly normal — just like his.

23

THEY talked all the way home. He told her he was divorced and she told him she had almost gotten married once. He said the worst thing about getting divorced was that everything seemed pointless. She said that was the worst thing about not having married, too. They arrived in front of the inn and he turned off the engine. He heard himself breathing in the silence that came right after. He held his breath and heard hers. He looked over at her in the nighttime wash of soft grays and lunar silvers. She looked over at him. They came together in a kiss that surprised them by its sudden gust of tenderness.

They got out of the car and started up the walk. Neither was eager to go inside. The indoor world seemed alien to them, and they looked in through the lighted windows like wild animals watching a campfire from the darkness of the woods. They didn't mind the darkness. They were part of it.

Let's go for a walk, he said. Let's, she said. In the rarefied air, the word, more sighed than spoken, with a touch of hot breath and darkly glistening flick of tongue across bared teeth, expressed pure, animal joy.

They set off for the harbor. The stars had lost their silver thistles with the rising of the gibbous moon. At land's end they came to the marina and went down on the wharf. Their footsteps were loud on the planks. The harbor waters were still as black glass. The white lobster boats rode them like sleeping swans.

Fran looked out to the unmanned light at the end of the break-water. Wilma had thought she heard howling in the islands from there. They crossed the sea wall where spray had frozen in sheets to the granite steps. Caroline went with him without a word, as if she knew where he wanted to go. The jetty was made up of an amalgamation of tailings from the quarry. On top the skeleton of the narrow-gauge railroad that had hauled cut granite to harbor ran out on the reach. The rails were long gone and the railbed mostly gone, exposing the bleached pilings, and the ties that had not washed or rotted away lay jammed and splintered among the rocks. They clambered out to where the gravel bed had washed out between the giant blocks. The water insinuated itself into the chinks, hissing and sloshing and undermining, always undermining.

They looked to the north, and slowly, like a photograph coming clear in developer solution, they made out the flats, the horizon of ocean, and the shadowy humps of islands ringed by wafers of shore. They heard the suck of the undermining sea, the wash of surf across distant gravel beds, the groan of estuary ice, and now and then the moan of truck tires far away on Route 1. And something else. Something so high pitched and faint it was impossible to tell if it came from far off or deep within.

Close by they heard footsteps. The harbor light came round and they saw a man picking his way along the rocks, coming in their direction from the reach. Fran recognized him by his thrifty movements, but Ed Hentov, eyes on his footing and his field of vision lowered by the hood of his parka, hadn't seen them. Fran called out to prevent a collision. Hentov looked up like a startled cat, big eyed, ready to pounce or scat.

Caroline broke the silence. "Ed, I think you and Fran have met."

Hentov looked at each in turn. "So you two have joined forces." Then chidingly, irritated at having been caught off guard — just like a cat — he said to Fran, "Hell of a place to bring a lady on a moonlight stroll."

"Lady?" Caroline said. "You must really be mad at us to use a word like that."

Fran said they had come to listen. Ed admitted that was why he had come, too. But it was no use, not over water. At such a distance water played tricks on the ear. As if by agreement they became silent, each listening to the echo of his own expectations. Then they started back. Ed and Caroline spoke of the days he and her father hunted together. Her dad knew the woods, he said. He had great patience. Fran felt her pleasure.

They climbed the sea wall to the street where the Blazer was parked in the shadow of the rampart. The cab light came on when Ed opened the door and Fran saw a rifle on the back seat, a powerful bolt-action piece with a flashlight taped to the barrel stock. The cat's eyes did not miss a thing.

"Some men jack coyotes," Hentov said, "some jack another man's private papers."

"Sounds like you've been talking to Mal Boulding."

"Was that tub of guts in on it, too?"

"Cut it out you guys," Caroline said. "You're spoiling my moonlight stroll."

"Sorry, Caroline. I'll get out of here and leave you two alone." He climbed into the cab and Fran and Caroline started up the street. In a minute or two the Blazer passed them with a beep.

"How'd your father die?" Fran asked.

Caroline didn't say.

"Wasn't a hunting accident, was it?"

"He had asbestosis from working in the shipyard during the war. He died of lung cancer."

It was reassuring to Fran, after his chat with Dr. Tagen, to learn that a Parker or Thomas could die a normal, all-American death.

They passed the last customers of the night coming out of the inn. The men recognized Caroline and said a respectful good night even though they had done more than their share of business. Inside, the taproom fire burned low with a heap of embers hissing on the hearth. Manly Howard was getting ready to close. He gave Fran a suspicious look. Manly had worked for Caroline's father.

"Care for something hot?" she said to Fran, stepping behind the bar.

"The hotter the better."

He meant this innocently enough. Now that he was indoors the memory of the icy jetty made him shiver. But Manly seemed to divine a different meaning. He looked Fran up and down in the way of short men in bifocals. Fran felt the urge to tease him, encourage his suspicions. Serve the busybody right. A glance from Caroline stopped him.

"This should keep you warm all the way home," she said pointedly, serving up an Irish coffee with an extra dollop of cream.

Manly cast down his eyes in shame. How could he have thought such a thing? Caroline was like a daughter. To atone for his vile suspicions he made a point of finishing up quickly and wishing the young people a pleasant good night. And as he locked the front door behind him on the way out he harbored not the slightest suspicion it might not be unlocked again before morning. Meanwhile, Fran harbored not the slightest suspicion it might be. He had been ready to torment poor Manly because he didn't think he was going to bed with Caroline that night. The look she gave him changed that. It did not say *don't tease Manly*. It said *don't give me away.*

They listened for the click of the lock. Then she came round the bar and he put his arm around her waist and they crouched together at the dying fire. She took a sip of his hot drink. It left a whipped cream mustache that she licked away with a long swipe of tongue. She hunched her shoulders in a shrug that said she knew she was undignified but that was the way she was and he better learn to like it. He liked it.

He took some cream on the tip of his tongue and stuck it out for her. She sucked it off and stayed for a kiss. This kiss was different from the one in the car. That one was romantic, this one was a matter of biology.

"Stay the night," she whispered. She didn't have to whisper. They had the long, dimming taproom to themselves.

"Isn't your mother's bedroom next to yours?" He whispered, too.

She raised sly eyes to the ceiling. "This is an inn, remember?"

They snapped off the lights and went into the lobby where she took a flashlight from the desk. They took off their boots before climbing the stairs. The guest rooms were unoccupied off-season and the only light and heat rose from the stairwell. His shiver returned. At the top of the landing she shined the light down the ell corridor where facing rows of porcelain doorknobs stood out like bulbous, chalky bones.

"We'll take the room at the end," she whispered. "It's over the fireplace."

She led him down the corridor. He felt disembodied, connected to the world of the living only by the touch of her hand. The farther they went, the colder and darker it was. A great sadness welled up in him, a penetrating sadness, as when we cry for dead loved ones in our dreams.

She opened the door and closed it as soon as they were inside to keep in the precious heat that had risen from the taproom below. She turned on the bathroom light so they could see and left the bedroom light off so they couldn't see too much. She turned down the quilt on the boxy, old-fashioned bed with the high brass posts. She turned to her lover.

He hugged her fiercely, lifting her off her feet, touching as much of himself to her as he could. There was nothing sexual in it, not at first. He wanted to break through, touch his soul to hers. Clothes, skin, and flesh got in the way. He wanted to strip them away and press his naked soul into hers and make just one. But he lost his way. The physical contact became the thing itself. The clothing itself became an erotic second skin, a prepuce.

"Good," she cooed. "Undress me." And sure enough he found his hands busy among the buttons at the back of her skirt. She stepped back and the skirt fell to her ankles. She sat back on the bed in her pantyhose and sweater with the slip riding up her thighs. He ran his hands up her legs and inserted his palms inside the waistband of the pantyhose and pulled them down. She leaned back on her arms and lifted her bottom to help, staring at his fingers webbed in the stretchy, sheer material. The sweater and bra came off next, leaving her breasts free and cool and the nipples erect. He wetted each with the tip of his tongue and blew them dry. How she trembled. Off came the slip, and the hands came back for the panties. She crossed her legs. "You first." She sat up and undressed him.

He watched her attend to him. In a swoon of wonder he marveled at the difference between the woman Steel Harbor knew by day and the creature at that moment depriving him of his briefs, her cheek the length of an eyelash from his nakedness. When she finished her work she lay back and caressed him, not with her hands but with words. She whispered the most marvelous things to him, sweet and obscene, in a voice that was not entirely her own. As if she were possessed, bewitched, and her words an incantation, a spell. His mind went all glitter and swirl like the dancing frost. Her legs parted and he was drawn down by invisible hands. The smell of her excitement ached in his throat. Until that moment everything had been slow, exquisitely, torturously slow, but no more. He pulled down her panties with such haste that the elastic snagged on her big toe and snapped back, but the other leg was free so he left the panties dangling at her knee and moved on her and she closed around him.

They made the beast with two backs, but, ah, sadly, with two souls. Never one.

24

JUST look at yourself. Are you trying to shame me in front of the whole town? It's bad enough his car is sitting out front for everybody and his brother to see."

Fran woke up to this coming from the other side of the bedroom door. Morning light, growing stronger by the minute, brightened the window. They had overslept and Mrs. Parker had the goods on them.

"I will not keep my voice down. What do I care if he hears me? I wish somebody in this house would. Honestly, I thought you were a sensible girl."

Caroline raised her voice for the first time. "I'm a woman, Mother."

"You're no lady, that's for sure."

Then he heard nothing. Either they had lowered their voices or murdered each other. He nuzzled the sheets where she had lain. They were still warm and he could smell her in them. And on himself. He felt easy and calm with a man's slow confidence the morning after. He felt sure, very sure of himself, and tender and playful.

The window brightened. It was darker inside than outside and long fangs of ice hung gleaming from the eaves. He imagined himself swallowed alive, looking up the beast's gullet through the mouth to blue sky, like the duck in *Peter and the Wolf* quacking down in the wolf's belly. He tried humming the part of the duck's stodgy oboe from Prokofiev. He couldn't get it right. The French horns he got right. They still sent a shiver through him.

Da-Da-Da-Da-Da-Da Dum Dum Dum Dum Dum, DA!

Caroline came in. All her beautiful coppery hair was cut off. What was left was cropped and wiry, like a big-eared boy with a cowlick. She was in the slip she had worn the night before and barefoot. The effect was waifish and wanton and underlyingly violent, as if she had done some unspeakable harm to herself. Her face had a stunned look, as if what had been done had been done by somebody else, an agent over whom she had no control. He decided not to ask why. In the first place he doubted that she could have explained, and in the second he felt that he was at the bottom of it, that what had been done had been done for him or at least because of him. He was the cause of some great change in her and she was suffering for it, suffering for them both, as in the pain of childbirth.

"Come back to bed," he said. He couldn't wait to get his arms around her. Comfort her. Handle her. Like a baby. Like a woman.

But she did not come. She stood between the bed and the door and looked at him with the palest eyes, the color of seawater in treacherous shallows. The yellowing light did that to them.

"Poor Fran. He wants to be in love so much." She reached up to twirl a lock of hair and her fingers snatched at nothing. Her eyes showed confusion, then awareness. She ran the hand over the bushy top of her head. A new sensation. "Don't fall in love with me. Don't make that mistake."

She gathered up her skirt and bra and pantyhose. As she bent over to pick up her boots he reached out and stroked her sturdy bottom through the flimsiness of her slip. She straightened up and glanced back at him, reluctant and sensual. She didn't want him and she did. She wanted him at night. During the day she denied him, denied her need for him. At night she denied him nothing.

"I'll take my chances," he said huskily.

She looked as if she would say something devastating. "There are clean towels in the bathroom if you want to take a shower. Excuse the mess in there." Then she left, barefoot and in her slip, carrying her bundle of dirty clothes.

Not a kiss. Not a hug. Not a good-bye. For some minutes he sat at the edge of the bed and marveled at her. Finally he roused himself and padded across the chilly floor to the bathroom. A pair of blunt utility scissors had been left on the rim of the sink.

Fine strands of reddish hair were visible on the porcelain surfaces. The wastebasket was full of a placental heap of the stuff.

Suddenly he felt that someone was behind him. He turned and found the bedroom empty, the door closed. The feeling was stronger than ever, however, and it occurred to him that the sense of a menacing presence or of being spied on or whatever it was — a strangeness certainly — came from the room itself. Why? He took in all the details that had been hidden by darkness the night before. The wallpaper with its pattern of bluebells and bulbs among a lush weave of tendril. The cedar chest at the foot of the bed with its antique iron lock. Th old-style brass bedposts, thick as the pipes of an organ in a college chapel. He noticed how the brass picked up the yellow light from the window and cast a watery reflection on the bare, waxed floorboards. He had dreamed this room. He had dreamed the stairway and hallway to it and the woman who brought him. There was no shaking the conviction that Caroline was the dream woman. The impression of certainty was bound up in the recognition itself. It should have pleased him — love predestined and all that — but it didn't. It sent a shiver through him the way the French horns did.

25

*D*R. *Phil Hallahan will be at memorial service for WS, Thurs 11:00 A.M., Interdenom Chapel, Orono campus. Says needs to talk. How about lunch?* — *Angie*

Fran found the note under his phone when he arrived at work. He went downstairs to look for Angela. She wasn't in the morgue so he went upstairs and checked the mailroom and switchboard. He went back to the newsroom and there she was at his desk writing another note.

She cringed when she saw him and jerked her head toward the fishbowl. Ray was at his desk in a haze of smoke talking on the phone. He saw Fran and his eyes got beady. Fran read his lips. *Call you back.*

"Too late," Angela said.

"What's this all about?"

Ray's door burst open in a puff of smoke. His ears were red as a rooster's comb. "Get in here, you two."

"Never mind, Angie. I think I'm going to find out."

It was the story Ray had taken away from Tommy and given to Fran. He hadn't stayed on top and it had broken big. It was a local story and the Portland and Bangor papers carried it that morning and the *Republic* hadn't. Ray was furious. He was also hungover, and that gave his fury an edge. He said he had a good mind to take Fran off and put Angela on. She'd been the one who brought the competition's stories to Ray's attention.

Fran's and Angela's eyes met. He saw how eager she was, how ashamed. She would have sold her soul — or his — for the break. It might have been different if they were lovers, but then they weren't, were they?

"Let her have it."

Ray was curious, clinically curious. "You heard the man, De-Gregorio. It's yours. Salvage what you can. Page one tomorrow morning."

Angela steadied herself against the desk. The cane wasn't support enough. "I'll get right on it . . . Ray." It was the first time she had ever called him by his first name.

"You'll do crackerjack," he said. "Now let me talk to Fran alone."

She avoided Fran's eyes on the way out, but the door clicked behind her with a finality that made her look back. He saw her through the plate-glass window. Her face was bleak with success.

Ray swiveled vertically in his chair, as if it were a rocker on an Oklahoma porch. "I'm worried about you, Scoop. I worry about my reporters when they give their bylines away."

Fran said it was the Steel Harbor story. He couldn't concentrate on anything else. There was satisfaction in the way Ray rocked. He'd thought as much.

"Quite a little girl you introduced Peg and me to last night. Niece of one of the suspects, isn't she?"

Fran said he knew where Ray was going. He'd been there himself.

"Then why in hell did you let yourself get personally involved? I ought to pull you off this one, too. Maybe I'll put Tommy back on the payroll and give it to him."

Fran's blood was up. His pride hardened. If Ray said another thing he'd quit. If Ray said anything at all about Caroline he'd shove his bald head through the plate-glass window — and then quit.

Ray didn't say another thing. He rocked. The chair squeaked with each rock. He stopped mid-rock.

"Take the weekend, but if you can't break this story open by Monday you *will* accept a new assignment."

Fran started for the door but Ray called him back. There was an embarrassed look on Ray's face. "You and Angela made such a good team that I thought . . . I hoped you two . . . Well, never mind. Take care of yourself down there. Yokels can be trouble. Ha, I ought to know."

26

THE university was over a two-hour drive, part of the way through the wilds of Waldo County, and the roads were bad and Fran was late. He arrived in the middle of the service and sat at the back of the chapel. He did this as quietly as he could, but everybody turned and looked back at him anyway. There were two groups of mourners and each kept to its own side of the aisle, like at a wedding. One group looked familiar. Wilma's features and mannerisms were parceled out among them. They were all in black. On the other side were academic tweeds and bright blazers and parkas. Dr. Phil Hallahan was with this group. His black hair hung greasy and unkempt over the back of a starched white collar. He had remembered to put on a clean shirt but not to wash or even comb his hair. Such were the inconsistencies of grief.

The service was protestant, with more talk and less ceremony than Fran was used to. A deanish clergyman was delivering a homily on something called con-so-lacy-ion. Boiled down, it was about why somebody as bright and good and young as Wilma had been struck down while there were so many wasters running around unscathed. The good dean didn't know either, and was saying as much, but so impenetrably he hoped the congregation wouldn't catch on.

Fran wasn't the only one with this impression. Hallahan had turned sideways, his brutishly handsome Irish profile heavy in the brow and jaw, and was staring at the stained-glass windows. The scenes were not religious so much as piously patriotic. The style, like the architecture of the chapel itself, was vintage WPA. Sinewy men in pigtails and knee breeches and bosomy women in aprons as vast as sails felled trees and built churches, killed and converted Indians, shot game and offered up Thanksgiving. Hallahan was gazing at the panel directly across from him. Fran couldn't see it from where he sat. Suddenly Hallahan looked around at him with a gruesome stare, his face bathed in roseate light. He looked as if he were suffering the flames of hell.

When the service was over he caught Fran's attention and gestured toward the Swanson family. He raised a finger to indicate he'd be one minute. Fran took the opportunity to get a look at the window Hallahan had stared at for so long. He came round into its full light and stepped back with a shock. A pioneer colonist in pigtail and knee breeches and carrying a blunderbuss shielded his wife in a big white apron and daughter in a little white apron from a pack of wolves. The family was fighting its way to the log church in the background across the snowy clearing. Underneath was the inscription,

> Behold, I send you out as sheep in the midst of wolves.
>
> Matthew 10:16

Fran went outside for some fresh air. Hallahan joined him a few minutes later. The rosy chapel light had masked his pallor, and to say that his waxy skin was the color of death was no exaggeration. His beard, eyebrows, and hair were luxuriantly black and coarse, as hair on a corpse is said to grow in the grave.

"Let's find ourselves a couple of whiskeys," he said, starting down the steps ahead of Fran.

He named a place in Bangor and Fran drove. They followed the frozen river into the bleak outskirts of the city and stopped at a renovated warehouse in the old waterfront district. The bar inside was all brass and brick and Tiffany glass, the kind of place California was lousy with. They sat at a corner table under a pot of philodendron, the broad, ear-shaped leaves bent over all the better to hear them.

"Human heartworm," Hallahan said after the waiter had brought their drinks. "I've been messing around with the life cycle of Nematoda and the analogy struck me as highly appropriate. Guilt is human heartworm. You aren't responsible, you had no way of knowing, there wasn't a thing you could do; but human heartworm is pernicious once it infects the host. I find that bonded bourbon is a satisfactory albeit temporary wormer." He took a long drink. "The side effects are prohibitive, however, especially after prolonged medication." He finished the drink and waved down the waiter for a refill. Fran was not half finished with his.

"I grew up in Riverston," he went on, chewing the ice from his glass while he waited for another drink. "My sainted mother resides in the family warren on Eglise Street. I get the *Republic* sent to me in Orono. I clued Wilma in on your original piece."

"You don't blame yourself for that, Dr. Hallahan?"

"Phil. Call me Phil." The fresh drink arrived and he paused to take a sip, a measured sip. He puckered up as if he were taking his medicine.

"You're missing my point," he went on. "I've been following your series — halfway decent writing for commercial journalism — and I have to ask you something."

Fran said go ahead.

"Have you come across — how can I put this — phenomena inaccessible to rational analysis and verification?"

"You mean ghosts?"

"Give me a break."

"What do you mean, then?" Fran was getting a little tired of Hallahan — Phil.

"Look, I have something to tell you and I don't want it in print. Does that compute?" The look of desperation intensified, along with a nastiness released by the alcohol.

Fran said he was listening.

Hallahan shut and rubbed his eyes. He brought his fingers together in a tent over the bridge of his nose. He opened his eyes directly into Fran's and began his account.

Tuesday night he was at his office on campus pretending to work late. What he was really doing was trying not to think, especially alone at his apartment. He and Wilma hadn't lived together, but her overnight things were there, a toothbrush and some underwear, his old L.L. Bean chamois shirt she used as a robe. "Booby traps," he called them.

So he stayed late dissecting roundworms and observing them through the microscope. Sometime after midnight — he didn't know exactly when because his watch had stopped — he looked into the eyepiece and instead of seeing the specimen he saw Wilma's headless corpse tangled in gear at the entrance to the tent, just as he had found her. He cried out and looked away. Hallucination, he told himself. He rested his eyes, changed lenses, and looked again. This time he saw the raven he had driven away from the head. It had already pecked out the eye on the exposed side of her face and was trying to roll the head over to get at the other. He shouted and ran out of the office.

He paced the hall and took deep breaths. That was when he noticed how cold it had become. He could see his breath. The thermostat for the floor was located inside the door to the taxonomy lab and he went in and switched on the light. The reading was in the sixties but it felt like twenty. He was about to switch off the light when he saw a dark red glow in the shadows at the back of the room. The rear counter served as the departmental museum and attic, and all sorts of specimens ended up collecting dust back there. He was afraid somebody had left on the gas jet of a Bunsen burner that would start a fire. As he went closer he saw that there were two lights, not one, bright and piercing like blood-red stars.

He recognized the wolf skull Wilma had brought in. It was lying on the counter with the upper jaw set to the mandible. The strange light seemed to be coming from the eye sockets. He hypothesized that the smooth orbital surfaces must have reflected light from the front of the room. He passed his hand across the skull, but no matter how he shaded it he could not cut off the light. Was the skull itself the source? He bent close to get a better look and brought a finger up to insert into one of the sockets.

The jaws creaked open and snapped at him.

He lunged back and threw his arms in front of his throat. The skull had resumed its inanimate state. The glow remained, however, brighter than ever. He had the feeling it was watching him — and had been ever since he came into the lab. He felt its hatred radiating in waves like heat from a furnace. On the cabinet shelf above the skull was a stuffed raven. He had seen it a hundred times, but now its glass eyes had picked up the glow and were staring at him, too, with cool, jeering, ravenish hatred. And then the other specimens. The mounted cormorant and the moose skull and all the others. Their eyes came on like Christmas lights. He backed his way to the door, stepped into the hall, and switched off the lab lights. Their eyes were still shining back there in the dark when he shut up the lab and locked the door.

He went home and got drunk, or tried to, but he was so wired up the alcohol didn't take. He stayed in his clothes all night in case he had to make a quick escape — in case they broke out of the lab and came for him. As soon as it was daylight he went back. The skull was on the back counter. It hadn't moved. The eye sockets were dark, as were those of the other specimens. He couldn't bring himself to touch it. He swept it into a paper bag with a yardstick and took it down to the waste disposal plant and threw it into the incinerator. He stayed until he was sure it was destroyed.

"It stunk when it burned," he said. "Like sulfur. Saltpeter." His eyes were wild. "Fire and brimstone."

He was suddenly very drunk. The whites of his eyes showed beneath hooded lids and he broke out in a clammy sweat. Fran was afraid he would pass out. The two drinks had primed the pump of a deep well of drunkenness that had been filling for several days and nights. Fran roused him and got him into his coat. He managed to get his arm stuck in the sleeve and punch down the pot of philodendron. He stared morosely at the smashed plant on the floor.

"Poor Phil," he said.

27

FRAN was glad to be rid of Hallahan. He was mad at him the way a parent is mad at a child for hurting itself. He was mad at him for his egotism, his self-pity, his wild grief, and wild drunken story. But most of all he was mad at Hallahan because he believed him.

When he got back to Riverston he telephoned his parents. First his father came on the line and then his mother on the extension. He hadn't talked to them since New Year's and they thought it was a social call.

"Dad, why did you and Mum decide to stay in Connecticut when you retired? You used to talk about retiring to Havenport."

Silence.

His mother broke it. People changed, she said. His father and she had lived out of state for thirty years and when it came time to go back they found it hard to burn their bridges. "All our friends . . . ."

"We've been reading you in the paper," his father cut in. They took the *Republic*, as they had all the papers their only son had worked for.

"You can guess why I've called, then."

They knew how dearly he loved the farm, his mother said, valiantly insisting on missing the point, but the house needed so much work. "And at your father's age . . . "

"I can guess," his father said.

Fran tried to make a joke of it. "Is there a curse on the Thomases or something?"

His mother answered. "All you Thomases seem to think so, and that amounts to the same thing."

Now dear, his father said — and well it's true, his mother said — and then they both said things, nettling and comforting. Fran would have liked putting a law into the books that allowed parents one telephone per household.

"Hey, folks, it's my nickel."

The truth was that his grandfather had become depressed toward the end, his father said. He wasn't himself. Fran had been away in the service and then in California and hadn't seen his decline. He stopped washing. He turned suspicious and hateful. He said things that made Fran's mother cry and his father so angry he couldn't stay in the same room with the old man. The ordeal gave them second thoughts about retiring to the farm themselves. It was way out in the woods, his mother added. No wonder the poor old fellow was so depressed. He was lonely and didn't know it.

Fran asked if wolves played a part in his depression.

"I'm getting off the line," his mother said. "When you're ready to talk about something pleasant I'll pick up the phone." There was a click.

"He said they were coming," his father said.

"When?"

"If he didn't die soon."

"Grampy didn't kill himself, did he?"

"Pneumonia, the old man's friend. Just as we wrote you. Your mother blames his pipes. You remember those."

They laughed together about Grampy Thomas's pipes, as black and crusty as the muzzle of an old cannon, and the tobacco, strong as gunpowder. They remembered the sparks flying and the black smoke that stained the white tin ceiling over the rocking chair by the kitchen window where he always sat.

"How have you been feeling, Dad?"

"Can't complain, Fran. I think the air's healthier down here for us Thomases."

The phone clicked. "I heard your father laughing. That must mean the coast is clear."

It was dark outside by the time he hung up. Winter darkness was another thing he had forgotten about in California. Out there the sunsets went on forever. Here, a reddening in the sky, then thud, like the closing of a Bible. He turned on the lights and the window became a mirror. He saw the child in himself, a dark little boy lost in the night.

The next number he dialed he had to look up first. He didn't know it by heart the way he knew his parents' number. Not yet.

Manly Howard answered. It was noisy in the background. Fran asked for Caroline and Manly said she was busy with happy hour. Fran said it was important. He didn't say who he was because he could tell Manly knew. Mrs. Parker had been right about the VW not going unnoticed outside the inn all night. "Hold your horses," Manly said.

"Uh-huh?" Caroline had picked up the phone.

Fran said hi it was him.

"Uh-huh," she said the way she would to a delivery man.

"I miss you."

"Not now."

Her end of the conversation was probably being overheard by a long line of men at the bar, and by Manly, busy with his bar rag; and perhaps even by her mother — on an extension. He said he was driving down to Havenport in the morning to look at the farm and wondered if she'd like to come along. She said uh-huh.

He heard a voice like a goat's bleating for a beer.

"You better let me go," she said.

"I'll never do that."

28

FRAN arrived at the inn midmorning. He had started out later than usual to give Caroline a chance to sleep. He crossed the lobby and knocked. There was no answer. He called out her name and knocked again.

"Can't you tell she's not there?" Mrs. Parker had come out of the coffee shop and stood sideways looking across herself at him. It was the stance she would have taken if she had been a member of a firing squad.

He asked if Caroline had left a message.

"She left, period."

But she was expecting him.

Mrs. Parker's mouth started open in a cruel slide, but something about him made her not say what she was going to. Her flat eyes had none of the gray or green that made her daughter's so volatile. They were blue and they had a shine to them, but it was the shine of serge that has been ironed too many times.

"If you're planning to spend much time with that girl, you'll have to get used to her disappearances."

There was in her voice a hint, the slightest hint, of an offer of alliance at Caroline's expense. It would be her tack if he became her son-in-law. The long-suffering mother in wry sympathy with the bewildered newcomer. Fran wouldn't have any part of it.

"Tell her I stopped by."

The mouth slid open after all. "If she was expecting you, she already knows."

He drove by Woody's and slowed down at the turnout. He thought of stopping to look for Caroline. He speeded up and drove on. Where he was going he might as well go alone.

The Star Route connected the seventeenth-century fishing towns at Penobscot and Muscongus Bays. It ran north-south across the peninsula over spongy tidelands and rocky hillocks, and for every mile there was a legend of a Viking ghost, an Indian massacre, or a lost Acadian maiden. He came over the top of the last hill and the white steeple of the Congregationalist church broke the plane of the crest. Havenport was even more of a backwater than Steel Harbor, but because it was twice as far from a major town it managed to support a few more local businesses. The only change he saw as he drove through was the new phone booth outside the IGA. The shiny metal and Plexiglas module was as out of place among the clapboards and granite as a space capsule touching down among aboriginal huts. The Star Route ended at the channel landing, where a half-submerged forest of rotting pilings was all that was left of the old fisheries.

He turned onto the narrow iron bridge that crossed the channel and his tires hummed on the grating. The sound was as familiar to him as the voices of his grandparents. The single-lane road down Thomas Head was plowed. There were no Thomases left, as far as he knew. They had all died off or moved away. The trees were shorter than he remembered, the road longer.

He came to the break in the stone wall that marked the lane down to the cove. There was no room to park so he drove on to the entrance of the farm. The driveway wasn't plowed. The new owners were summer people, all right. He could see the house down past his grandmother's cedar grove, a saltbox with a carriage barn across the yard. They had once been white. The new owners had painted them salmon.

He walked down to the barn and forced his elbow through a pane of glass at the back window. He reached in and released the hidden latch and forced up the sash. He hoisted himself inside and found the flat-head spade hanging where it always had and climbed out with it. He shoveled out a parking place at the driveway entrance. He felt in the right. Anybody who painted Grampy Thomas's house salmon deserved worse. He heard the old man's sigh of approval in the cedar boughs.

With his car off the road he went back to the entrance of the lane and waded into the woods. The snow was to his knees. He had always come at Christmas, the time of ice storms, not January, the time of deep snow. The stone walls were troweled with thick copings of it, and the old cellar holes were like craters of the moon. At the little cemetery the granite gate posts leaned in towards one another and the gray slate tombstones poked up through the drifts like buoys in a rolling sea. The major's marble stone with the brass marker stood square as an old soldier. There were no footprints. The dream had been only a dream.

He might as well have gone back. He didn't. He followed the lane to the cove where ice-edged streamlets trickled down fissures of frozen mud. There were no footprints here, either. He looked back at the winking woods. No beckoning, wolf-eyed snow queen in a snowflake gown. Dreams were dreams. He should have gone back. The cliff face with the pine trees on top still looked like a Mohawk Indian to him. Beyond was the blustery bay. He walked out along the frozen rim of the cove and the sea blow picked up. It slapped at his clothes and stung his face and made his eyes water when he looked into the teeth of it. A point of land appeared beyond the cliff. As he walked farther out more came into view. It wasn't a single reach of land but a chain of islands. He recognized the forested hump of the largest. Funny, he didn't remember the Channel Islands being visible from Havenport.

He went back not by way of the cove lane but straight to the tidehead. Knee-deep in snow again he clambered up the highest hill to see if he could locate the farmhouse. The pastures were overgrown but there did seem to be a clearing through the brush in the right direction. He took a step and stopped. Even after he recognized the rocking chair he didn't quite believe it was there. It shouldn't have been. His grandfather's favorite chair, up to the seat in snow, should not have been on top of the hill.

There was no mystery about it. He could picture some Boston lawyer relaxing out here on a summer afternoon with a tumbler of Cutty over ice and a fresh *Christian Science Monitor*. The weather had stripped the varnish and bleached the wood and in a year or two the chair would be kindling. He tried to lift it but the rockers were frozen to the ground. He was tired from the long walk through deep snow and from the wind pushing him around on the shore so he cleared off the seat and sat down. The snow came up to the undersides of his thighs. He looked down the cove, past the cliff, and across the choppy bay. The islands were farther south of here than they were north of the Steel Harbor jetty, but the view was better, more complete. If he had a good pair of binoculars, like the ones his father had given his grandfather one Christmas, he might have sighted the boathouse.

A chill entered him and grew more severe and localized until it was like a dagger of ice in his bowels. It doubled him over before it passed and left him with knowledge. He knew that the new owner had not put the chair out here. He knew how his grandfather had come by his pneumonia.

The clearing through the brush led directly to the farmhouse, as by now he knew it would. He drove back to town and stopped at the futuristic phone booth and put through a call to Ed Hentov's office at the paper company. Mr. Hentov was in the woodyard and couldn't be reached at the moment, his secretary said. Fran left his name and said he wanted to talk to Mr. Hentov about using his boathouse that weekend.

29

AFTER the desolate places he had been that day, the city at twilight was a welcome sight. Lights were coming on in the suburban mall and downtown in the stores and offices, in the wooden apartment houses and brick schools and mills. On his own street the front window of Jimmy's Market was brightly lit. He saw Jimmy inside at the cash register and batty old Mrs. Connors, wobbly in her orthopedic shoes, on the sidewalk out front.

He parked the VW and climbed the two flights of stairs to his landing. His door was open a crack. The stairwell bulb showed long, splintery scratches and the knob was bent. He kicked in the door to the wall to make sure nobody was behind it. He flicked on the light and went into the kitchen and took the butcher knife out of the drawer. The table had been tipped over and his portable typewriter and file folders were on the floor. The photostat copy of the wolf hunt, his notes, Woody's drawings, and Wilma's photographs had been torn up and scattered. He went into the bedroom and found his bedding in tatters, the mattress harrowed to the ticking. His pillow was ripped and there were feathers everywhere.

He sneezed.

Across the street Jimmy was ringing up Mrs. Connors' groceries: a loaf of day-old bread, a stick of margarine, a tin of baking cocoa, five cans of kitty dinner . . .

Fran came in out of breath. He asked Jimmy if he'd seen a stranger go into his place during the day. Jimmy couldn't say that he had.

Fran felt a tug on his sleeve and looked down into Mrs. Connors' cloudy, wide-set eyes.

"Ask me," she said. "We saw the young man go right in the door."

When had that been?

"This forenoon. The small ones and I were looking out the window at the big crow in the tree and he went right in."

"The crow, Mrs. Connors?" Jimmy said.

Fran asked what the young man had looked like.

"He had excellent posture. Didn't slouch like most young people nowadays. And clean-shaven," she added, squinting at Fran's bristly face. He hadn't shaved that morning.

What color hair?

"How should I know? He was wearing a hat. It's cold out there."

Jimmy helped Mrs. Connors to the door with her shopping bag. He and Fran watched her toddle past the window outside.

"Wouldn't take what that old girl said she saw too serious, Mr. Thomas. She's got the cataracts."

On the way back to his apartment Fran saw a Blazer that hadn't been there before parked next to the VW, and when he came over the landing he found Ed Hentov standing in his living room.

"You all right?" Ed said.

Fran told him he'd been away when it happened.

"Anybody see who did it?"

Fran told him the half-blind cat lady down the street saw a clean-shaven youth with good posture enter the building that morning. Ed gave him a look.

Fran took him into the bedroom and showed him the slashed mattress. Ed got angry, angrier than Fran, in fact. He clenched his fists so tightly the knuckles turned white. "You going to call the police?"

"It's my story," Fran said. "So far it's an exclusive."

They went back to the other room and set the table and chairs upright. Ed picked up the typewriter and the carriage slid off and banged on the floor. He put the pieces on the table. Fran found two Pabst Blue Ribbons in the refrigerator, the last of the six-pack he had bought the afternoon he was assigned the story a week — a lifetime — ago. Ed took one like he was being polite.

"I got your message," he said. "I'm coming, too."

He said he had been thinking along the same lines since the night on the jetty. They'd take his sleds. And his rifles.

"Think I'll need one?"

"Your friend had the right idea about a night blind. Predators learn to hunt at night around man. What she didn't take into account is that they lose their fear of man. They know when to hide, but they know when somebody's helpless, too. Like she was."

The animals they were dealing with were mongrel, coyote for starters, with wolf bred in for fight and dog for impudence. They'd need the rifles. Especially when the pack got wind of the bait.

Bait?

There was a slaughterhouse in Friendship that dressed Ed's game. He was dropping by on the way home to pick up the hindquarter of a freshly killed horse the butcher was saving for him.

Fran thought of the hamstrung ox.

"I have a little Mossberg .30-30 you can zero in before we start," Ed said. "I'll carry the Remington you saw the other night." He looked at the typewriter in front of him on the table. "I know we live in different worlds, but I'm willing to give yours a chance if you'll do the same for mine."

Fran followed Ed's eyes to the typewriter and read the trademark. Remington. Different worlds, indeed.

After Hentov left, Fran tried the other tenants in the building. An unmarried couple — unmarried to each other that is — lived on the second floor. She was a nurse and he was a shift worker at one of the mills. They lived their lives at odd hours. The vacuum cleaner was heard at midnight, a drunken argument at nine in the morning. Only the young woman was at home. She had birdlike bones and pale skin and dark rings around hungry eyes. She said she hadn't been home that morning. Her boyfriend had but he was at work now. Wouldn't he like to come in for a drink?

The family on the first floor was French-Canadian. The husband spoke English with an accent that sounded less like French than Transylvanian.

"We don' know, I'm *certain,*" he said, standing between his plump, much younger wife and Fran. A skinny little girl ran to her mother and said something in French.

"*Attendez! Attendez!*" the woman said as her husband was about to close the door. They spoke together rapidly.

"Ma girl hear bell — *tintement* — today in the hall.'

"*Comme Pere Noel,*" the child insisted.

"Like Father Christmas," the father smiled, his mouth full of sharp, crooked little teeth.

Fran went upstairs and checked the damage to his lock. The deadbolt had been forced through the doorframe. He found red flecks of something in the splinters. He picked up a speck on the tip of a wet finger and smelled it.

Iron. Rusty iron that smelled like blood.

He put a chair against the door for the night and went into the bedroom and turned over the mattress and made the bed. He and Ed were starting out early. They would be up all the next night.

He called Caroline before he went to bed. He hadn't intended to. He intended to punish her for standing him up. But as it got late and cold and quiet he realized he was only punishing himself.

"Give the poor girl room to breathe," Manly Howard said. It was Friday night and things were going full tilt in the background. Fran stuck to his guns and pretty soon Caroline was on the line.

"Sorry about this morning," she said right away.

"Why didn't you leave word with your mother?"

"I did."

It hadn't occurred to him that lying might number among Mrs. Parker's faults. She struck him as the kind of woman who could do more damage with the truth.

"When can we be together?" she said so softly he almost couldn't hear. A wild need for her went through him. He saw her, placid and cool, under the scrutiny of a bar full of attentive men.

He told her about his and Ed's plans. Then, rough and tender, "I know you can't talk, so listen. I'll be back Sunday. I'll be cold and tired, and I'm going to come in there and take you upstairs and make love to you, and I don't care if your mother and Manly and half the town see us."

She did not hang up and she did not speak. She stood there taking it in front of all those thirsty men.

"I know what you are and I know what you want. I know what you need. No more of this good-little-girl act. No more hide-and-seek. I'm through seeking. I've found you."

He hung up on her.

30

DAWN caught him on the road. First it wasn't there and then it was, and although he took notice right before and right after, he didn't actually see it break. Driving the road had become second nature to him — first the suburban heights, then the river valley and paper mill, the forest with the long scar of clearing for the power lines, the curve where he had gone off. He saw the imprint in the snowbank where the VW had struck. Then came the unmarked driveway to Ed Hentov's. The house was less imposing by daylight, more like a home designed by an architect with a little money to throw around than a castle in the woods. Ed and his older boy were out front loading the first of two snowmobiles onto the trailer hitched to the Blazer. The sleek, bullet-nosed machine lunged up the ramp, the engine shrill as a harpy.

Fran stopped and got out of the car. "Need some help?"

"We got the first one up by ourselves," the boy said. He wouldn't look at Fran.

"Eddy," his father said.

"It's not fair."

"Say hello to Mr. Thomas."

"Hello, Mr. Thomas."

"Hi, Eddy," Mr. Thomas said.

The boy ran into the house.

"He wanted to come with us," Ed said.

"Why can't . . ."

"His mother," Ed said without letting Fran finish.

He started the second machine and showed Fran how to work the throttle. The sled stabbed forward onto the trailer and Ed cut the motor. The blue smoke lifted and the air buzzed with silence.

They went into the kitchen where Barbara was making breakfast among stainless steel appliances and butcher block counters glazed by sunlight. The light drained her olive complexion. Her black hair shone like coal.

"We meet again," she said to Fran, her resonant tones up an octave.

They sat down in the sunny breakfast nook to stacks of buckwheat cakes, fresh grapefruit, and coffee. The boys joined them, and the husky stationed himself a strategic distance from the table.

"How in the world did you let Ed talk you into going?"

Barbara's voice could have shattered crystal. It went to the back of Fran's eyes like a toothache. He said the trip was as much his idea as Ed's. In fact, he had made the first contact. Ed said that was so, but he would have gone anyway and she should be thankful to Fran for not letting him go alone.

"Thankful that two of you will freeze to death now instead of one?"

"Oh, Mom, there's a stove in the boathouse." Eddy's frustration bore witness to an earlier battle.

Young Barry was the only happy Hentov this morning. Blissfully and with intense concentration he shoveled huge quantities of syrupy pancakes into his bud of a mouth. His forehead glowed with the effort of chewing and his cheeks dimpled each time he swallowed. Fran struck up a conversation with him to lessen tension and soon they were discussing prehistoric man. Barry wanted to go to Africa when he grew up and follow in the footsteps of Richard Leakey.

"I wasn't any older than you when I read about his discovery of Ginjanthropus in *National Geographic*," Fran said.

"Pardon me, Mr. Thomas, but that's Zinjanthropus. Mary and Louis Leakey, Richard's mother and father, discovered it."

"As I said, it was a long time ago. The Olduvai Gorge, right? Earliest man ever found."

Barry cleared his throat. "Not quite, Mr. Thomas. Zingy was

an australopithecine. *Homo habilis* is now considered the first true man."

"What gave him the edge?" Fran said in his best hard-nosed reporterese. "What single development made everything that followed possible?" (That ought to stymie the little wiseacre.)

"Bipedalism," Barry said without hesitation.

Fran felt himself getting angry. Were a thousand millennia of human achievement reducible to an animal learning to walk on its hind legs — a circus trick? Barry wasn't a little boy any more. He was avatar of the age.

"Man's hands were freed so his brain could think up stuff for his opposable thumb to do," Barry went on, running his own thumb through the syrupy residue on his plate and licking it. "Man became a hunter instead of a scavenger. Up until then he wasn't much more than a featherless buzzard."

Barbara left the table. Without a word, without the squeak of a chair or the sound of a footstep, she rushed from the room. Ed went after her. Dog tags jingled through the house as Bullets followed his master.

Poor Barry, avatar no longer, began to cry. "What'd I say? Eddy, what'd I say?"

"Who knows?" Eddy folded his arms in disgust. "She's been acting weird all morning. Maybe she's on the rag."

The boys slipped away and left Fran alone in the sunny breakfast nook. A clock ticked somewhere out of sight. It sounded like an old clock, with drowsy silences between loud ticks. After a time Ed came back. He picked up his cup and splashed the cold coffee into the sink and poured some hot. He took a swallow and splashed the rest into the sink.

"Ready?" he said.

"How's Barbara?"

"Later. Let's go down to the game room."

They went downstairs to a basement den. Fran couldn't tell if game referred to the pool table and dart board or to the racks of antlers studding the paneled walls. Ed unlocked the gun closet and selected two rifles from a half dozen rifles and shotguns. He handed Fran the lever action .30-30 and took a box of cartridges from the drawer. He showed Fran how to load and chamber, how to release the crossbolt safety. Fran had not handled a rifle since the army, a plastic and suitcasy M-16, and the Mossberg had a wicked feel to it, stubby as a shillelagh, balanced as a bow. They went out back where he zeroed in three rounds on a target posted to a bale of hay. The reports clapped clean and the cordite tickled his nose. The shots printed tight but high. Ed told him he was anticipating the kick. Relax, he said.

"This is as relaxed as I get."

"Aim low, then."

Ed was nervous, too, but in him nervousness was converted to stillness — as if he were saving it all up for something.

The horseflesh was in the garage, wrapped in a sheet of plastic and bound to a snowmobile pull sled. The carcass included the full hindquarter from the broken ends of rib to the sticky tail. The garage smelled like a meat locker. They hauled the sled outside. The load shifted on the way up the ramp and the hoof flung loose and gave Fran a nasty rap on the wrist. It was the hoof of a draft horse, broad and shaggy.

They wedged the sled between the snowmobiles and Ed went back and brought out a sloshing five-gallon gas can. Blood, he said.

"Won't it freeze?"

"We'll thaw it on the stove and lay down a trail before dark."

There was a note of desperation in Ed's voice that hadn't been there the day before. At Fran's he had merely been determined. Fran brought up the scene at breakfast.

"This is hardly the time or place," Ed said.

"Barbara been having bad dreams?"

Ed's eyes bored into Fran's skull to see where his brain was getting its information. "Have you had such dreams?"

"Not the past few nights, but the night Wilma died I did, and her boyfriend seems to have, too." Pause. "You want to tell me about Barbara's?" He knew he didn't.

"Typical nightmare," Ed struggled. "Sense of helplessness and thinking you're awake when you aren't. The usual."

"Something Barry said reminded her of it?"

"You know how women are."

When they were ready to leave, Barbara came outside to say goodbye. She had thrown a coat over her shoulders and hugged her elbows. Ed went to her and Fran heard him say that she shouldn't have come out, he would have come in. They embraced. His padded arms coiled around her, and her hands fluttered out from under the constriction and lighted on his back. Her diamond glinted in the sun.

They turned arm in arm and she beckoned to Fran and he approached them. Her jaw was set and she smiled as though through tears, but there were none, just dry dark eyes.

"Dreams are only dreams," he said to her.

"Ed told you?"

"Leave him inside or he'll follow us," Ed yelled to the boys, who were on their way out the door with the husky pushing past. They grabbed the dog by the scruff of his dense coat and stuffed him back into the house.

At the last minute the family came together. Hugs and horseplay. Corny jokes everybody laughed at. Barry put his arm around his mother and Eddy held the door of the Blazer for his father, and as the men drove out of the dooryard Ed glanced up into the rearview mirror at what he was leaving behind.

31

THE upper story windows of the Widow's Walk Inn blinked in the morning sunshine. Fran wondered if Caroline were still in bed, sleep clinging to her like a fragrance. He made out the window of the room where they had spent the night. The icicles hanging down outside were thicker and longer than the ones hanging down the other windows.

They drove past to the marina and turned upland at the jetty. The four-wheel-drive bucked them up the washboard snowpack of the old railway bed. At the top, a huge, free-standing iron flywheel dominated the entrance to the quarry. They drove into a ravine of scarred cliffs and shattered boulders. Already that morning a few children from town were skating at the quarry sump. The hillside planed off along the north face where the wind had heaped an impassable drift. They stopped and unloaded their machines.

A snowmobile is a chimera, a beast of disparate parts. The throttle is mounted on the handlebars like a motorcycle. The two-stroke engine bubbles with the sweet blue fumes of an outboard motor. The caterpillar track belongs to a small bulldozer, and the skis and nose have been swiped off a bobsled. The clothing is equally provisional. In the crash helmet and nylon wind suit, cuffed gloves and zippered boots Fran looked part downhill racer, part astronaut. Ed showed him how to nurse the choke, how to absorb shock in the thighs instead of the spine, how to shift weight to tighten the turning radius. Fran did a turn around the Blazer to get the feel of the ride and pulled up behind the lead rig. Ed put on his helmet and mounted, and when he was set he pulled twice at the cord of an imaginary whistle and they revved their engines and were off.

They eased over the crest of the drift and swept down into an alder swamp. Branches swatted them as they skirted the juniper and burdock. Seed tufts exploded in drifting armadas from cattails cut down by their skis. They broke powder and skidded across black ice. They climbed the oak ridge that separated the fresh-water swamp from the estuary marsh. Their machines struggled in the deep snow beneath the oak trees. The engines chugged, threatening a stall, then rose like wild laughter as they came down the other side and burst onto the flats.

Ed slowed the pace. The drone of engines melded with the rush of wind. After a while it was like the silence of the deaf. With trancelike fascination Fran watched the little dumb show played out before him. The spinning caterpillar track of Ed's machine spewed silver bits of ice dust, every turn and jostle exaggerated by the pull sled to wide veers and bucks so that the cargo of horse-flesh was kept in a state of violent motion. The hoof came loose again and hung over the rear of the sled. As the joints froze the leg stiffened out so that by the time they reached the narrows, the hoof pointed at Fran like an accusatory finger.

They pulled up at the ice bridge. Ed's rucksack and slung rifle made him have to swing his whole torso around to look back. He gestured that they should cross one at a time. Fran saluted. He saw himself salute in the reflection from Ed's visor. He waited for the first machine to clear the span, then followed in its tracks. He did not look down but saw the water out of the corner of his eye. It was deep, winter-clear, waveringly sunny below. He felt weightless. He saw himself underwater looking up at the sun. What peace, what cool clarity.

Then he was aware of time, that a block of it he couldn't account for had elapsed. He had come across safely. He felt let down.

They rounded the point and the boathouse came into view down the crescent of shore. They leaned landwards to offset the icy plane. Halfway there Ed gunned his engine and shot ahead the rest of the way. By the time Fran arrived Ed had dismounted and unslung his rifle. The door hung open with the padlock locked to the jimmied hasp. With the random unexpectedness of a dream

Ed chambered a round and stalked barrel-first inside. Was he out of his mind? Fran looked back toward the ice bridge. Too far. He had a vision of Ed turning on him, of the big Remington shattering his spine and driving splinters of bone through his lungs and on out through his chest as he tried to escape. He saw the snowmobile career across the water, skip on its skis in a slow full turn, and sink with him slumped over the handlebars.

Ed came out of the dark doorway with the rifle in the crook of his arm. "Sorry," he said, squinting against the sunny snow. "I forgot the police were here last week."

"Who else did you think it was?"

"I said I was sorry."

The boathouse had two rooms connected by a low door that was like a trap door standing upright. The camp section had a plank floor, potbelly stove, bunks, and two witches' windows — square windows mounted diagonally into the ridge ends of the roof. The boat shed had a dirt floor and no windows. It smelled of bare earth and gasoline. An old wood-hulled launch was berthed on the cradle. A crack of light beamed through the darkness along the top of the sliding boat door. This was the only other entrance to the boathouse and was locked shut by both an iron pin wedged between the runners and by floe ice shelved against the base and seized up solid.

Forty paces north along the shore was the standing trunk of a dead spruce. The top had been blown off long ago leaving twenty feet of stump and the main branches. Ed drove the stiffened carcass up under the tree and he and Fran tightened a noose behind the hock, looped the rope over a high limb, and hoisted the great joint of meat into the air. It weighed as much as a man.

They looked back to the boathouse window, a safe eight to ten feet off the ground. The opposite window faced the south shore. The channel was to the west. They would have one blind side, the woods east beyond the door.

"We'll know about it if they show," Ed said.

"Will you shoot?"

"As many as I can. How about you?"

Fran didn't know.

Ed's throat tightened. "When you see the way blood excites them and the way they fight over the meat, I wouldn't be surprised if you gave that little bush rifle a workout."

They closed off the shed and built a fire, and by the time they stowed their gear and sat down to lunch, the camp had warmed up — at least compared to the ten degrees above zero outside. Barbara had packed sandwiches of rare roast beef on corn rye. Fran never tasted anything so good. He wolfed his down. Ed must have been just as hungry, but ate his slowly — more slowly than he would have if he hadn't been hungry, Fran thought.

The stove was hungry, too. It chewed up softwood in its red teeth at a ravenous rate. The woodbox was empty. After lunch Ed sent Fran on a fuel run. In the meantime he'd scout around on foot.

"Don't get lost," Fran said. "When it gets dark I'm locking that door and not a god damned thing's getting in."

He took the ax but not the rifle. He wanted to stay calm, and carrying a gun made him feel like he might have to use it. He hitched the sled to his snowmobile and circled back along the narrows to the cove he and Wilma had found, where he remembered a stand of blighted birch. Some of the trees were so rotten that one swing of the ax split the wood and brought an avalanche of bark and red pulp down on his head. Others were iron-hard, the blade barely creasing the tough yellow pulp and the blow vibrating through the handle into his bones. The footing was equally treacherous, crusty enough to support his weight one step, giving way into deep powder the next. More than one armful of wood went tumbling. The forked limbs knew how to flip themselves out of the sled when he tried to stack them. One ornery old knee of hornbeam went for his shins. The ropes were stiff and wouldn't knot properly. He lost a glove in the snow when he took it off to tie them. He went wild finding it. Lose a glove this weather, you'd soon lose the hand.

By the time he was ready to go the sun was cool as the full moon and dropping rapidly toward the mainland. He slipped the ax under the ropes. He heard a twig snap nearby in the brush and slipped the ax back out. He heard a cough. It was so much like a human cough that he thought Ed had come looking for him. He was ready to call out when a young buck stepped from the thicket, the buck he and Wilma had seen. Two smaller deer stepped out as well and pulled up short behind the erect white flag of the first. All three froze, not looking but seeing, aware, so still, hearts racing, full of hot life.

The cooling snow ticked.

Fran moved first. He put the ax into the sled. At once the deer set off in a dainty trot along the shore to the ice bridge. Several more came out of the woods down the line. Hooves clattering, ears and flags high, the procession crossed the span in single file and glided across the flats into the moonlike sun that had just touched the distant mainland treetops. The wilderness took on the colors of a watercolor painted by a child too young to know better — yellow sky, purple trees and blue snow, a vermilion bay.

Ed had beaten Fran back to the boathouse. As they carried the wood inside Fran told him about the deer. Ed's eyes burned like sunset.

"They know," he said.

The young fire snapped up the dry, dead sticks of pine. It sizzled the birch, charred the ironwood, and chucked angry embers against the grate. Ed put the gas can on the stove. Soon blood frothed at the spout and the handle was too hot to touch barehanded. But night was quicker than fire. The witches' windows had turned to black diamonds.

"Bring your rifle," Ed said.

They went into the woods. Fran carried the .30-30; Ed lugged the can of blood. He led them to a deer yard he had scouted earlier and began dousing the snow. The hot blood steamed like piss and left dark melt stains; and the smell of it, rancid and sweet, sent a devastating shiver through Fran. He cocked the rifle. The double click of milled steel was the most comforting sound he'd ever heard. They worked back towards the boathouse, their pace quickening as the can got lighter. Fran kept his distance, repelled by the thought of getting splashed with blood. He knew he would soon be safely inside with the door barred, but the idea of a trail of blood leading directly from the deer tracks to his pant leg was too much for reason. They came out of the woods near the bait tree and Ed splashed the last of the blood against the carcass.

A scolding shriek — and a big raven flapped out of the tree away into the night.

Fran let out a little shriek himself. He looked to Ed for reassurance and was shocked to see what terror had done to his partner's face. This man of authority, this father of sons, was reduced to a helpless baby. The pale light of the rising moon exposed a face with the lines smoothed out, the eyes wet and huge, the mouth softened with drool.

"Ed?"

Like talking to a baby.

"Ed!"

Hentov spat violently into the snow. He wiped his mouth on the back of his sleeve. "Let's go inside."

The camp was dark and the fire low. Ed turned on his flashlight and found the kerosene lamp, which he filled, lit, and trimmed. Fran shook out the grate and brought the fire growling to life. Ed lowered the crossbar on the inside latch. Thus in light, warmth, and shelter, and heartened by the little rituals of providing themselves with these basics of civilization, they regained their composure.

"Sorry about the way I acted out there," Ed said. "Inexcusable."

"That's the second time you've apologized to me today."

"Big fellow. Didn't see him until he flushed."

Fran remembered Barry's talk of buzzards at breakfast — right before Barbara left the table. "Did a bird figure in Barbara's dream?" he asked.

Ed fetched the Remington across his knees and assembled the cleaning rod. "It wasn't her dream. It was mine."

32

FRAN sat in the rafters with his legs dangling in the darkness below and his elbow propped against the sill of the cockeyed window. Outside, the stars twinkled off the black water and glowed in the snow. The hoods of the snowmobiles had the sheen of patent leather. The night sky was immense. Constellations swarmed like schools of fry in the shallows of the universe.

"Awake?"

"Awake," he lied. He stretched himself awake and blinked across the exposed rafters at Ed's silhouette against the opposite window. Ed didn't seem to be having any trouble staying awake. His dream of the night before might have had something to do with that.

Ed was not the kind of man who remembered dreams. He had said so with something like pride, as if dreaming were a weakness and talking about them self-indulgent. He hadn't forgotten this one, though, nor had he been able to keep from telling Barbara about it. He awoke fighting for breath in her arms.

A hunting trip. For deer rather than coyotes. He'd gone alone. Once in the woods he threw away his rifle and clothes, one piece at a time — his cap into the pond, his shirt on a bush. When he was naked he took to stalking his prey on all fours. What freedom he felt, what power. He outlasted a ten-point buck. (A nine-pointer, really, one of the main points having been broken off. Strange, remembering that.) He brought the animal down with his bare hands and broke its neck in his teeth. The blood ran hot down his chest. A shadow passed over and a great dark bird landed on the rack of the dead deer. It eyed his bloody nakedness and he felt shame. He tried driving it away but each time the bird perched again on the antlers. He became enraged and pounced on it and wrung its neck. The sleek head drove at his face. The beak snapped up his tongue. The wings spread huge and came clapping over his face and stifled him with dusty black feathers.

Fran saw it as if he himself had dreamed it.

Ed went on talking, opening up as he probably never had to another man. He talked about his father, how he emigrated from Russia after the First World War, alone, both parents dead, a boy no older than Eddy. Driven by a ruthless desire to make good and by some secret hatred of his race, he shunned the company of Jews, learned English, and worked his way up in the pulp and paper business, a Gentile's business. Late in life he married the mill superintendent's daughter, a stout, blond-haired, blue-eyed girl of Norwegian extraction. As a child Ed's curiosity about his paternal heritage was systematically dampened, and he was encouraged to embrace the traditions and excel in the pursuits of his maternal relations. In the end the father succeeded so well that he and his son were strangers to one another. The old man was an anti-Semitic Jew, but still a Jew, and he had raised a son who wasn't particularly anything. An American, his father liked to say. With pride. And with pain.

That had been hours ago — dark, cold hours. Fran raised his wrist to the window and looked at his watch by starlight. It was past midnight. The stars throbbed. They seemed to tinkle like bells, a sparkling sound.

"Bullets?" came Ed's voice.

There was scratching at the door, an anxious yip.

"He's gotten loose and followed us."

"I didn't see him come up the shore," Fran said, scanning the swath of silver that led back to the ice bridge. He felt the joists shake as Ed let himself down. The flashlight came on and beamed at the door. A single hoarse bark came from beyond. Fran drew up his legs.

Ed raised the crossbar and opened the door a crack. The husky's snout pushed into the light and then the rest of him squeezed through. "Boy, he's cold," Ed said, roughing him up affectionately.

"He's come a long way," Fran said.

The animal did an amazed double take, looking up at Fran,

looking up again. He hadn't known about the man in the loft. The resourceful eyes took in the situation. Fran felt like the crow with the piece of cheese in the fable.

Ed rekindled a fire from the old coals and put a cot blanket on the floor by the stove before climbing back to his post. The husky circled and made a nest and dropped with a jingle of tags. The camp was quiet again, and as the fire died, cold again. Timbers creaked. Ashes tumbled. Ice groaned. And between, long stretches of throbbing silence.

"Listen."

"To what?"

"Listen."

Fran listened and heard noth— no, something. A low moan rattled his fillings as if the sound were coming from inside him. But it wasn't. It came from far away, one of the outer islands, and was followed — accompanied — by a higher, shriller wail on the opposite shore. A third, in the middle both in pitch and location, and all three rose in wild harmony. Then the night exploded in star burst as the husky raised a shattering howl.

Ed jumped down and muzzled him with his belt. The dog whimpered and tried to rub the muzzle off between his paws. "Easy, fella." The dog would not be comforted.

The howling had stopped. Fran waited with senses cranked up to animalistic keenness, breathing through his mouth to hear better, watching his field of fire a little from the side to see better in the dark. He had difficulty keeping his imagination in check. The darkness, the silence, the cold, and the soft insulated clothing deprived his senses and his mind began making things up. Like the two boys standing below the window. He shook himself and saw that they were really the two snowmobiles. But the impression lingered. They had been dressed in old-fashioned Norfolk coats, woolen caps, scarves, knickers. Ah! He had to touch something solid. He took off his gloves and felt the .30-30 all over, like a blind man.

Hours passed — or minutes. His sense of time, like his physical senses, had become distorted. Time had lost its way and was wandering in circles. He felt vertigo, not falling down but falling back, as in a feverish dream.

The rafters shook. Ed was moving.

"Gotta pee."

"Not outside?"

Ed chuckled. "No, not outside. I'll just step into the shed." He dropped to the floor and the husky rose to greet him. "I don't think there's anything out there, anyway."

"You don't?" Fran had the sense he was looking down into the murky depths of a pond.

"They've been warned off." Ed slapped the dog on the rump. There was more in his roughness than rough affection. "That's why somebody should have stayed home."

He opened the fire door and stirred up the coals with a stick of pine, then tossed it and some birch bark into the stove. He held his wrist close to the new flames. "Got the time, Fran? My watch stopped."

Fran held his watch up to the pale starlight. Still twelve something-or-other. Impossible. He stared hard at the second hand. "Mine's stopped, too."

Ed opened the shed door and shone his flashlight inside. The blackness swallowed the light. As cold as the camp felt, the chill that scuttled in from the other room was far colder. And damp as well, if air that is below freezing can be damp. Ed stooped and passed through. The husky followed. Soon came the splatter of hot urine on frozen earth. Fran thought of the bloody melt stains in the snow. Ed had not been worried about getting splashed with blood. His boots were soiled with it.

Ed said something. Fran couldn't tell what. It was in a mildly surprised tone of voice, the surprise of recognizing the familiar. *Of course,* the tone said, *why didn't I see before?* What he said was harder to figure. (Menorah, it sounded like.) Then came a popping sound, like the bursting of stays, and then a snarl and scream. The snarl and scream were all mixed up in each other so that it was hard to tell where one picked up and the other left off. And loud. So loud that Fran's eyes seemed to dry out in the sockets and roll out of his head.

Clack.

The scream got weak and gurgly.

Clack.

A groan.

Fran dropped through the air. His stiff legs hit the floor like pickup sticks. He managed to keep his balance and hold onto the rifle. He even had the presence of mind to release the safety. But he couldn't for the life of him remember if a round was chambered. He cocked the lever and heard the ping of the wasted cartridge against the floorboards. Five left.

The flashlight lay beyond the trap doorway in the moon of its own light. No sign of Ed or the dog. Fran crouched at the entrance but didn't go through. The animal could come at him from any direction, even from above if it were in the launch.

"Ed?"

There was movement. He heard a voice, unintelligible but human. Then a scraping sound, and beneath the ribs of the berthing struts hands appeared in the circle of light dragging their broken body behind. The head looked up and tried to speak. It made gagging noises. The tongue had been ripped out.

"Take my hand." Fran reached in just as the body was jerked back into the darkness. But not before he saw the flash of fangs.

And fired.

The explosion rang round the boathouse and filled the air with brimstone. He cocked and held fire. No response this time when he called out.

The flashlight had been knocked back along the keel of the launch and had come to rest shining on the spike that held the boat door shut. No way out that way. The husky was cornered.

Fran stepped back and patted around for the lantern. He knocked into it hanging from the cupboard. Then he couldn't find matches. He seemed to remember a box by the stove — on the other side of the camp. He moved along the wall, not daring to cross in the open. As he passed the front door it shook against the crossbar.

"Mr. Thomas? It's Eddy. I've come for Bullets."

"Get away from the door, Eddy." Fran took aim at the square of darkness in the shadowy wall. He was afraid the dog would charge the sound of the boy's voice, but there was no movement, no sound, from the shed. "Wait a second, Eddy. I'm coming out." He reached behind him to raise the crossbar.

Why didn't the boy call to his father?

The door rattled the crossbar. "Open up, Mr. Thomas. It's cold out here."

Because he knows Ed's dead.

That was not Eddy out there. Fran almost doubled over with fear. He realized that he was the one who was cornered. He glanced up to gauge the distance to the loft. The instant he took his eyes off the trap door he was aware of something hurtling at him out of the darkness. He let go the Mossberg and lantern and leaped, caught a pair of joists and swung his feet over.

Clack.

The back of his snowmobile suit was ripped away and something crashed into the wall. His foot slipped as he stood up.

Clack.

A crushing weight clamped onto his boot and pulled him down hard on his tail bone against the joist. The whole roof groaned. The weight swayed and twisted and clamped, and as he braced his free foot and reached back to get a better hold, his hand fell across the Remington. He rammed the barrel down the length of his pinned leg and when it struck something that wasn't foot, he pulled the trigger.

Silence.

A silence out of which came the crack of bone — as pain

telegraphed through to his hip — and a tightening, clamping growl. He threw the bolt of the unfamiliar gun and this time it went off. Detonated. He was flung free. The sudden release of pressure was like a miracle.

Clack.

The sleeve was torn from his arm. Warm blood trickled down his fingers. He scrambled to his feet and pressed close to the wall. He threw the bolt. Where was it down there? Hazy beacons of starlight beamed into the depths of the camp from the high windows. Stools like submerged stumps and the table like an underwater boulder wavered below in the murk. Something hunkered over there by the wall. He felt the scrutiny of fiery eyes, the insult of a grin bloody with his blood. He fired, threw the bolt, fired again. The boathouse shook.

Now there was new light, red and smoky. He had shot the stove, shot away the jack-o-lantern grin of the grate and scattered hot embers beyond the piece of boiler plate the stove sat on. The floor planks were unsealed, and coals had lodged in the chinks and fallen through into the dry mulch beneath the camp where they smoldered. By the new light he saw that the animal was not below. It must have returned to the shed, wounded perhaps. In any case, it would not attack now that the man in the rafters had a gun and there was fire and light. But there was also smoke, more and more of it, and if he stayed put, he risked suffocation like a sparrow in a barn fire. Already his eyes had begun to water and his throat to burn. He knocked a pane of glass out of the window with the butt of the rifle and frosty night air poured through. He put his mouth close to the opening and breathed deeply.

The moon had set, but that made the stars all the brighter. The bait hung undisturbed in the tree. There wasn't a sign of life. The carcass swayed slightly. Funny, because there was no wind, not a whisper. The carcass twisted slowly around, and instead of a joint of meat he saw a bareheaded man in a frock coat and riding boots hanging by the neck. The neck was stretched twice normal length, the head bent almost at a right angle to it, eyes shut, tongue distended. The face was black as the boots. Fran closed his eyes. When he opened them the hanged man's opened, too.

He spun away from the window and scurried like a spider across the web of beams to the other side. Flames licked up through the floorboards and edged along the walls. He peered out at the snowmobiles, sleek, black, and poised, pointing unimpeded down the chute of shore to the ice bridge. He dug into his pockets for the key.

A snarl, but like a voice, like Ed's voice, like laughter, boomed from the shed. Fran dug for that key. Fire enveloped the trap doorway like a flaming hoop, the kind the tiger comes through. The center was strangely dark, as if there were a darkness that light couldn't penetrate. Waves of superheated, oxygen-depleted air rose around him. The cool key was in his fist. He cried out for joy. A cry from the darkness echoed his and went on after his stopped. First it was just like his, then it mocked his, and then it turned to singing — slurred, merry, complacent, lost.

> *K-K-K-Katy*
> *K-K-K-Katy*
> *I'll be waiting at the*
> *K-K-K-Kitchen door.*

His dreams were revealed to him. He saw Sam Comstock die. He saw Wilma Swanson die. He saw that their deaths foretold his own.

All hell howled. By the light of burning walls he saw his tormentor for the first time, saw it emerge bone-white and steaming from the black trap doorway and spring into the rafters for him. Up it rose through fire and smoke, no husky, no mortal coyote or wolf, but a hideous, unnatural thing, hairless and skinless and by all rights long dead, with eyeless sockets glowering and lipless, gumless teeth stinking of the boneyard.

Fran fired the big gun from the hip and it spun him back. He lost his footing and was on the way down when he set his good leg to the joist and drove himself through the window. It gave way in a shower of splintered wood and glass. Down he tumbled, the rifle lost but the key safe in his fist. He mounted the snowmobile before he had quite stopped falling. The key fit. He remembered the choke. The engine started at first crank, trembling, surging with power impatient to be transformed into speed. He opened up full throttle and the machine jerked forward and died. He had flooded the cold engine.

That was when he saw the eyes. In the darkness along the wood-line he saw half a dozen pairs ablaze in reflection of the burning boathouse. The one inside had flushed him for the others.

He turned the key and the engine started, frail this time, congested, wracked by an oily cough. He nursed it to health. Meanwhile the eyes pressed closer and the one trapped in the fire raised a deathly howl. He opened the throttle one-third and pushed off into the long shadow he and his machine cast before the flames. The eyes pushed off, too, in file along the woodline. At half speed they had no trouble keeping pace. In fact, the leader outdistanced him and was gaining an angle to cut him off. He opened up full throttle and this time the engine did not stall. The snowmobile exploded forward, front end rising, track biting in. He shut his eyes against the rush of subzero air blasting into his unprotected face.

Clack.

He took a blow to the shoulder that came close to knocking him out of the saddle. The cloying rank of fetid, meaty breath raised the hairs on the back of his neck. He opened his eyes in time to avoid the channel and aimed the bullet nose of his ma-chine at the ragged profile of spruce on the point. He ran without lights down the silver snowpack between the watery darkness and the hard, black wall of trees. He felt labored breath hot on the back of his neck, the nick and snap of fangs at his ears and wrists. He heard a horror of hungry groans and snarls and slavering yips above the screech of the wide-open engine. The point loomed ahead, coming on faster and faster as he swooped in. The machine planed under him as he made his turn onto the crusty narrows ice. He sensed a drag, a slowing, a lightness and unresponsiveness in the steering skis. The load had shifted, with more weight to the rear. There was only one explanation. He ducked.

Clack.

A tuft of hair was yanked from the back of his scalp and he breathed in the newly familiar putrescence of the charnel house. One of them had mounted the pull sled. He leaned into the handlebars right and left and the sled fishtailed violently. He felt the load lighten. He had lost his passenger. But the sled kept right on waggling and jackknifed and the whole rig planed into an uncontrollable skid. He threw his weight to the opposite side. Tree trunks whizzed past, ice sparks glanced off the side-scraping skis, a grin of malevolent triumph floated before him. Then — puff! — into a glimmery fog and out again, and for an interminable instant he was vaulted into the sky among the vast wheeling streak of stars.

Am I dead at last and my soul set free?

The snowmobile hit the water at a velocity that drove it well beyond the bank, hitting, spinning, hitting again before sinking abruptly with an equally abrupt cessation of engine noise. The night rang with silence.

A smoky mist with a reddish tint hung low to the water. The surface was black and feathery smooth, churned below by an undertow of current running out faster than the tide. Fran bobbed to the surface. He filled himself with sweet, cold air before his waterlogged clothes and boots dragged him under. Up he came a moment later, hands cupped and paddling madly until his shoulder blades burned. Down below he felt his legs nudged out from under him so that he hung aslant in the water. He was aware of a hissing sound, not loud, but all around, the sound of nets seined through water. The tide was taking him out to sea. He fought against it and was soon out of breath and had to do the dead-man's float to rest. He opened his eyes underwater. Deep down in the dark green he saw a fisherman in a sou'wester casting a net for him. The spidery net and oilskins gave off a phosphorescent glow. The dead man's face was grim, set to the task, eyes as round and unblinking as a fish's.

Fran kicked against the drag and swam cross-current. But in which direction? Sea smoke hid the shore. For all he knew he had gotten turned around and was heading back to the islands.

"This-s-a-way," came a voice, close.

Another trick? He was too exhausted to be careful, almost too exhausted to care. He swam toward the voice until flailing arms struck bank ice. He was grabbed by the collar and hauled on his belly out of the water where he lay gasping. The ice felt dangerous-ly warm.

"Get up."

He opened his eyes and saw a pair of rubber galoshes. Several of the buckles were jammed or missing with ruptures of pant leg bulging out. He was lifted to his knees and let go of, and he slumped back on his heels with his frostbitten hands in his lap. He raised his stunned gaze to Woody Parker's face. It looked big as the Indian face on the sea cliff, and as high up. The eyes glowed like those he had seen on the island.

He tried to look behind him, but the hermit seized his head in both hands. "No," Woody said, "not if you don't want to end up like me."

"I've seen them."

Woody searched his face and let go. "Poor little Caroline," he said.

Fran grabbed hold of Woody's hand and pulled himself to his feet. He turned around. A pack of skeleton wolves looked on from across the channel over the pall of mist. Tatters of mummified skin hung from naked bone or stretched drum-tight across a rib cage or peeled back from ivory teeth. One was headless, though it paced restlessly along the bank with the others and held up its stump of vertebrae as if the loss of a head were no great inconvenience. It hit him like a slap — what had happened to the head.

The eye sockets of the others — the eyes having long since rotted out — flickered with the tainted mist. The light could not have come from the boathouse fire, far in the background and dying, but seemed to emanate from the ice bridge itself. He had come close. The bridge loomed above the narrows not two dozen paces upstream, glimmering an auroral red, as if sea lamps had been buried in the ice. He made for it and the pack followed along the opposite shore. In the pre-dawn stillness the myriad little clicks and clacks of bone against bone went right through him. His teeth began to chatter.

The glow was cold, faceted, like blood crystals in the snow, rubies, Mars. More aura than actual light, the ghost of a light, yet it did its job. As he stood at the edge, one of the pack charged, snapping with ferocious yanks of the head and threatening to bound across. The creature pulled up short at the bridge and backed off stiff-legged, cracking its jaws and casting a covetous glance at the man just out of reach. Its eye sockets flared brightest when it was nearest the barrier and there was a stench of singed hair. The phantom flames of the old watch fire held the phantom wolves at bay, loathsome bones joined by the sinews of vengeance and quickened by hatred, maws opening through to ruined gullets so that flesh eaten fell undigested to the snow, leaving them forever hungry. He understood that what they really fed on was the dark blood of human guilt. He had not escaped them.

A ripple of excitement stirred the pack. The dreadful things pressed close as they dared and grinned. His damaged hands and crushed foot throbbed, but far away, as if they were somebody else's. The blood gurged from his head. His vision spun until the earth stopped turning.

"Fixed proper now," clucked the hermit, half insane himself. He trotted over and hefted the unconscious body across his shoulder. "S-s-save his life, anyhow, even if his mind's gone." He started for home. "The devils."

The body came to life. It twisted out of the hermit's grasp and raced to the bridge. Woody cried out and gave chase but stopped at the edge, wringing his hands and clucking furiously as Fran lunged across to the island. He was immediately surrounded.

Gasping for breath, heart pounding in his ears, shaking so hard that the rime crusted to his clothes and hair rattled, Fran cried out, "I know who you are."

All movement — all the terrible clatter of bone against bone — stopped.

"You're me."

He held out a frostbitten hand to the teeth of the nearest skeleton. It shook its head as if in a violent sneeze and shrank back.

"But who am I?"

They answered him by their transformation. For him they became beautiful lost creatures, keen and shining. The headless animal was now whole and in its eyes was a look of great suffering, but of indelible autonomy, too, and for an achingly sweet instant immortal spirit recognized itself and knew that it was timeless in time and changeless in change, that it would forever be and had forever been.

The ultimate trick? Had the wolves, which appeared to each victim in the form of his worst fears, appeared to Fran as his great hope? That question, that doubt, did not cross his mind. Good thing, because if it had, he would have been torn to pieces.

The alpha male, formerly the headless skeleton, now its winter pelt a lustrous black-tipped silver, withdrew to high ground and let out a low, throaty howl. The circle around Fran broke and reformed up the bank around the leader. The wolves nuzzled and nipped one another, fawned and bullied, accepting and asserting their places in the pack. Watching them, Fran felt that he no longer had a place. How could he go back after the things he had seen?

No sooner had he thought this than a woman, nude, silver like starlight and soft like moonlight, appeared at the edge of the woods. The wolves made way as she glided down to him. She was like Wilma Swanson, even her hair was sleeked back in a braid, but a flawless Wilma limned to perfection. The scars on her face were gone, the eyes were untroubled by compassion. She stopped an arm's length away and gave him a smile that filled him with longing and disquiet.

Come with me, she said without saying. *I am the woman you dream of.*

She took a step backward and he took one forward. Her smile turned rapturous. She took another and so did he. He was helplessly drawn to her, but felt powerful in his helplessness, like a male animal captured by the scent of estrus. Her scent was keen as frost, pungent as disturbed autumn earth. With accommodating slowness she started for the woods, casting sly eyes back at him over a bare shoulder. The coarse braid hanging down her back switched at her buttocks.

He did not take another step, because in the twist of hip and dip of shoulder he saw — not Wilma — Caroline. He saw her as he had last seen her, in the slip that clung to her as she turned and looked at him before leaving the blue room over the hearth. He saw her dreamy perplexity, *her* longing, *her* disquiet, as if she knew even then that she would lose him.

A flicker of predatory impatience narrowed the phantom's eyes. She turned, displaying the supple charms of her beauty to full advantage. There was a tensing of powerful muscles beneath silken skin. She approached, her yellow eyes devouring his, her tongue lolling from heartlessly perfect teeth. Then her mood changed. She relaxed, seemed almost amused, wry, and reached out and stroked his face. He felt the delicious thrill of her caress as her fingertips brushed his eyelids, cheeks, and lips.

She gave him a knowing little smile and dropped to all fours and was a lean gray wolf. Without wasting any more time on him she trotted back to the others. A yearling let out a whimper. Then with the silver and black animal in the lead the pack struck off in a line up the shore and disappeared into the darkness of the woods just as the darkness itself dissolved in the light of breaking dawn.

33

FOR a long time after he woke up he followed the bluebells across the wall, and when he shut his eyes he still saw their gracefully burdened bowing. He was safe in the blue room over the hearth and he was alive. These things astonished him. It was afternoon, socked in with winter fog, the kind of afternoon it was good to be sick on if you weren't too sick. He was pretty sick. His hands lay beside him in bandages. His foot was in a cast. He remembered Dr. Tagen having to cut away the boot because the foot had swollen so. The tooth marks went right through the rubber and skin into the bone. Mal Boulding had put the boot in a plastic bag, the kind he kept Sam Comstock's vodka bottle in.

He heard Caroline's footsteps in the hall. She was making noise being quiet about it. She knocked and he said come in and she tiptoed in — as if he had said come in in his sleep — and placed a tray of orange juice and buttered toast on the nightstand. She had on a white blouse of rough cloth and a silky aquamarine skirt that cast her eyes in the same color. Her hair was less raggedy. It had been trimmed and washed and brushed to shining. Its shortness showed off her slim neck and shoulders, and as she bent over the bed she reminded him of a bluebell.

"Is today Monday?"

"Yes."

"I was pretty sure."

"How do you feel?"

"Like a kiss."

"Good sign," she said, but he didn't get his kiss. "Hungry?"

He raised himself on his elbows and she propped up the pillows. He could handle the toast on his own but needed help with the glass. He looked at her as he drank.

"I don't mind," she said, anticipating.

"Something wrong?"

Her eyes were unhappy.

"I could make other arrangements," Fran said.

"With Angela?"

He smiled. "You're jealous."

"She's in love with you."

So much for the smile. The two women had met the day before at the hospital. Caroline drove him bundled and splinted to Riverston after Dr. Tagen had done what he could. Flat on his back on an emergency room examining table he phoned Ray. Good old Ray. He came right down and brought Angela with him. She blew into that hospital like she owned the place. She was an old hand there and knew the doctor on duty and the nurses and asked any number of impressive medical questions. The doctor was concerned about the patient's right hand. The rest of him would mend okay but it was too soon to tell about the hand. For the time being he needed rest and fluids — lots of fluids, because frostbite sucked tissue dry like a burn. Angela said the patient could stay with her. The two women sized each other up. It was up to him, Caroline had said.

"I'm not in love with her."

"Finish your juice."

"I'm in love with you," he managed before she stuck the glass in his mouth. "Or would be if you'd let me," he added when she took the glass away.

She went wall-eyed, like flash photos you see of high-strung horses. "You should have gone with her."

"Sleep here with me tonight."

She put the tray in order. "Mal wants to talk to you."

"Caroline."

"We'll see."

He listened to her going. The inn was so quiet he heard her all the way to the bottom of the stairs. The diminishing footfalls made him drowsy. Somewhere a faucet was dripping. Each drip made him drowsier, as if drops of his own blood were dripping away. There was a knock at the door. He knew he had been asleep because he hadn't heard footsteps.

"Enter." He expected Caroline with Mal Boulding.

It was Dr. Tagen in an ancient suit, carrying a relic of a medical bag. "I've come to change the dressing."

Fran's wrist was taken up by cool, scaly fingers, the reptilian skin and metabolism of old age. "Humph, reg'lar."

The doctor sounded put out with Fran's pulse for being so perversely normal. Blood pressure next. The cuff fattened around his bicep like a black leech. "Ha."

"What's wrong?"

The shaky hands dismantled the antique sphymograph, then pincered Fran's jaw between thumb and forefinger and moved the head from side to side. "Never seen frostbite streak before. Looks as if you'd been scratched."

"Is it bad?"

The doctor ignored him and unwound the gauze from the left hand. The skin was gray and cracked, the cracks flecked with scales of dead skin. Except for the absence of liver spots the hand looked as old as the one that held it. But the flesh was supple and the joints unswollen and flexible. The doctor — and Fran watching him closely — breathed a sigh of relief. The gauze came off the right hand next. The best had been saved for last. Fran saw something that looked more like a piece of meat than a hand. Bald, angry blisters were raised on several knuckles and the cuticles had turned black at the stubby ends of swollen fingers.

"Edema," Dr. Tagen said as if Fran deserved it.

He set about swabbing away the dead skin. Hot tears ran down Fran's cheeks and mixed with cold sweat. The pain was like no pain he had felt before, exquisite, beyond any threshold he would have thought possible to bear and remain conscious, and yet not only did he remain conscious, he seemed to acquire a heightened sensitivity that opened doors to new realms of pain. In a vision he saw the golden eyes of the she-wolf. They were Caroline's eyes. She had come in with the chief.

"Bet that smarts," Mal said. His face was flushed and his clothes gave off the breezy odor of the outdoors. His boots were muddy.

Caroline would not look at Fran until the worst was over and his hands were being dressed in fresh gauze. She remained by the door, arms folded beneath her breasts, hugging herself, and when she finally did look at him it was with resentment.

"Part of your story checks out," Mal was saying. "We found the bones of a big dog in the ashes with Ed's body. Charred some, but when I fit the jaws to your boot, the bite lined up perfect with the tooth marks. Problem is, the Hentov dog never left the premises. Saw him up to the house this morning. Alive and kicking."

"The animal in the boathouse was one of the pack," Fran said.

"But you said Ed took it for his and let it in. How's a man going to mistake his own dog?"

Fran couldn't say.

"Another thing. This story about a pack. We haven't found a one of them."

"They go into the ground."

"They got a den out there?"

"They go back to being dead."

There. It was out. He had tried telling them the day before, both Mal and Ray, but he hadn't had the strength to face their disbelief. He knew the signs. How many times as a reporter had he pulled back when an unreliable source stepped over the line of credibility? He watched Mal go through it now — the noncommittal stare, the palm at the back of the neck — but with one difference. Mal was a cop, and in him disbelief translated to suspicion. His eyes glittered with it.

"Ed was killed by a pack of wolves slaughtered on the islands almost two centuries ago." Now that he had started he couldn't stop. "See for yourself tonight. You'll be safe as long as you don't cross the narrows. But be careful, they can influence your thoughts." He sniggered like a wretch. He sounded crazy even to himself.

Mal turned to Dr. Tagen. "Hysteria, Doc?"

The old man had been sitting quietly in the chair by the nightstand for several minutes. "No, Malory, the truth."

He turned to Fran, whom he had startled out of giddiness. "If I had any idea what Miss Swanson or you and poor Edward had in mind I would have spoken up. I expected each incident to be the last." He paused and looked at the chief. "I can't blame you for not believing him, Malory. It's the reason I've kept silent all these years. There are supernatural forces at work. Will you hear me out?"

Mal rubbed the back of his neck.

"You have to take off your cop hat for this one," Fran said.

Mal's mustache moved once like the flap of wings to indicate he'd smiled. "I'm listening."

Caroline edged into the room and sat on the lid of the cedar chest. She worried her hair throughout Dr. Tagen's account.

ǀ   ǀ   ǀ   ǀ

"The winter of 1924 I was a young physician trying to establish a practice here in Steel Harbor. The town didn't have a doctor, and for reasons I'll go into shortly, a small practice off the beaten path suited my needs.

"We had a bad spell the first of the year, and at the worst of it a fisherman named Collins was found dead on Brave Boat Island. The corpse was brought to my office, frozen stiff. A puddle of salt water thawed out of the clothes but I didn't find a drop in the lungs. There were some nasty wounds that looked like dog bites. Collins' dory was found adrift in the channel. His body was found above the tidemark. The evidence indicated he'd taken a dunking and was set upon when he made shore. Loss of blood and hypothermia sent him into shock and his heart failed. It seemed clear that feral dogs were the culprits. They abounded in those days because summer people had a habit of leaving half-grown pups behind at the end of the season. I submitted my findings and put the case out of mind.

"A day or so later I was called here to the inn to look at young Woodrow. His mother — Caroline's grandmother — said nightmares were bothering him and that he was waking up in the middle of the night screaming that wolves were trying to eat him. It didn't take long to diagnose hysteria. The little bugger was frightened way past normal childhood fears. I only hoped we weren't dealing with dementia, as well. I gave him a bromide to help him sleep, but that was no long-term answer.

"I took the case to heart. The Parkers were the first important family in town to put their trust in me, and I needn't tell you how important such a connection is for the new doctor. There was another reason, too. You see, while at medical school in Cambridge I suffered a nervous breakdown. We were so ignorant then. Brutality and prejudice compounded the suffering of the mentally distressed. After recovery my moral as well as mental fitness was called into question and I was nearly barred from taking my degree. I sought out a rural practice to hide my past as much as guard against relapse.

"Woodrow was calm enough next morning to describe the incident that lay behind the nightmares. He had been skating with his friends at the quarry pond. Sleet had fallen shortly before the big freeze that year and the boys found that they could use their skates on the glare crust. They skated all the way to the estuary where the other boys turned back and Woodrow went on alone. When the afternoon light began to fail, he turned back, too, or thought he had. Instead, he came smack up on the channel. Ice had formed across the narrows and a fire seemed to burn down inside it. He had mistaken the glow for the setting sun over the mainland. He said he had the strangest feeling about this. He felt that he had been tricked. It was then that he heard howling in the islands. He tried to flee, but couldn't. The howling grew louder until a pack of wolves came bounding toward him along the shore. They rushed the ice bridge but didn't cross. Only after he saw that they could not pursue him did he find the strength to flee. He never skated so fast in his life.

"I asked how he could be sure the animals were wolves and not dogs. He knew, he said, because they looked like what he had always known they would. You can guess that I surmised the boy had been frightened by the dogs that attacked Collins. He was only twelve or thereabouts but big for his age and he hadn't run. His initial shock saved him. Off their home ground dogs seldom attack a grown man standing still. The fire in the ice I ascribed to salt-water phosphorescence or even something the boy dreamed up under the influence of the sedative. I could account for everything except his extraordinary fear.

"After another night I took him off sedation and the nightmares returned, but with a new and alarming twist. He said the wolves were calling to him, trying to lure him back, and he was having a hard time not giving in. I could not conceal the dangers of such a development from his parents, and recommended institutionalization for his own safety. How your grandmother cried, Caroline, when I told her. In those days the common name for a mental hospital was the insane asylum.

"Nightmares can be contagious, and I began being troubled by dreams undreamt since my own breakdown some three years before. During that terrible time shadows haunted me. I dreamed of them at night and during the day the most innocuous shadows filled me with dread. You've heard the expression, 'He's afraid of his own shadow.' In my case that was literally so. The return of my old phobia shook my self-confidence and I had second thoughts about my diagnosis of young Woodrow. Had I condemned a perfectly sane child to a mental institution? There was one way to find out.

"I waited until after dark and didn't tell a soul. I went by way of the quarry, walking in bitter cold through the woods and across the flats. At the narrows I found the bridge Woodrow had described. There was no fire, but I didn't intend crossing in any case. The ice was too slippery. I remember thinking that such a buildup could occur only during the coldest of winters. The channel's width, the current, and the salinity of the water were against it.

"As long as my mind was busy with such matters I felt no danger. The night was beautiful in its stark way. The air was so clear that the moon seemed to have moved nearer the earth by half. Then I became conscious of my breathing. I couldn't shake the notion that something nearby was breathing in unison with me. When I inhaled, it inhaled. When I exhaled, it exhaled. And when I held my breath, so did it.

"I had been looking at the moon over my shoulder and all at once faced forward. I saw only my shadow cast across the ice bridge. I looked at my watch and found that it had stopped. I remembered that the waterlogged watch I found on Collins' body had stopped at the same time. A quarter past twelve. It gave me a shiver. Somebody must have walked across my grave.

"I examined my shadow more carefully. It began at my feet and stretched across the ice to the island, but there the slant of the neck and the length of the head gave it the look of an animal standing on its hind legs. I moved my head to the side to break up the illusion. It was only heightened. In half profile the pointed ears and snout were distinctly canine, and points of light appeared where the eyes belonged. When I stepped aside, my shadow broke away from the other and there were two. I looked behind me. There was nothing to cast the other. It just stretched down out of the moonlight. I walked downshore and the other sank to four legs and followed. There was no doubting its bestial nature then.

"I had the sense it was trying to communicate with me. My terror gave way to fascination and I stepped to the edge of the channel. The tide was up and chucking under the ice. The points of light looked at me and then at the water. The shadowy head nodded slowly. Suicide had crossed my mind more than once during the bad time. I thought of myself as a stoic. Death seemed an acceptable, at times preferable, alternative to life. If the symptoms were unbearable, the only reasonable thing was to put an end to the disease. Death awaited each of us in the long run or the short, so why endure what needn't be endured? Why suffer when suffering was meaningless?

"It wasn't so much that I was thinking these things, you understand, more that I was receiving them. Futility weighed me down like wet clothes. I caught myself leaning over the bank and pulled back, only to lean again, much as someone nodding off starts awake and then drifts back to sleep. I saw others. They detached themselves from the shadows of the woods and swept across the snow to the edge of the water. Finally, what had to happen — what they wanted, and perhaps what I wanted, too — happened. I slipped and fell and came to a stop with my heels in the water. Part of me didn't care. Part of me wanted to let go. But I resisted the temptation not to resist. What gave me the will? You may find this difficult to believe. It was my dead mother. She appeared to me. She spoke. She warned me against them. Lys and Skygge, she said in Danish, the language she spoke at home when I was a boy. 'Light and Shadow. Know the difference, my sweet son.'

"I inched my way up the bank until I could stand, and then I turned and walked away without looking back. I knew they were there on the shore watching me. I could hear their pacing, the scraping of their claws on the crust.

"It did not end there, of course. I had the boy to consider. I had to weigh his welfare against the possibility that I'd be disgraced. I took the half measure of asking his father to go with me to the islands without mentioning my earlier experience. I said I wanted to find out if feral dogs had frightened his son. Your grandfather was only too willing, Caroline, desperate as he was to grasp at any straw.

"We were held up by the January thaw, which came that year in driving rain. Oh, how it rained, for days, and then everything froze solid in the February freeze. By the time old Aston Senior and I were able to reach the estuary it was not the same place. The snow was gone and the melt-off locked in a hundred ice ponds. The marsh grasses were exposed. The ice had broken up and the narrows were free. We stayed out half the night, but nothing turned up. The feeling of otherworldliness I had been so aware of the first time was gone. My watch kept perfect time. When we got back to town, Aston Senior couldn't thank me enough for troubling so over the boy. I felt like a hypocrite, but without proof how could I have told him or anyone else what I had seen?

"My patient here will tell you, Malory, that the history of these parts has much to do with recent events. History is my passion. It has been a way of coming to know the enemy. My dogs represent a similar strategy. I know people think I'm peculiar keeping a pair of big dogs named Lys and Skygge, but now when I hear the scraping of claws on the stairway late at night coming toward my bedroom door I can believe it is them and not the others. I never married. It would have been unfair to the poor woman who shared my bed. I am haunted to this day. In little ways; horrible little ways. I never see my midnight visitors. You might say they stick to the shadows. And not once in all these year have I passed Woodrow on the street without admitting to myself that I deserve haunting. Each time I wonder if the long-term effects of his trauma might have been lessened by my telling the truth. I don't know. I do know that I cannot stand by and allow another young man's future to be jeopardized now that there is no proof of what he's told you."

I　　I　　I　　I

No proof, Fran thought. The fog and Caroline's sheer skirt and the dripping he now recognized as icicles melting outside the window and Mal's muddy boots — the thaw had come. By now the ice bridge would have collapsed and been swept to sea, and the dead were dead again for five or fifty or a hundred years when a new worst winter in memory bridged the gap between the mainland of our lives and the islands of our dreams.

He turned to share the moment with Caroline but she had left the room.

34

THE next time he woke up it was after dark. A muffled crash woke him. He listened but didn't hear it again. He felt immensely rested. He was hungry. His body was sore in every muscle and joint. These things told him he was on the mend. He needed to urinate but it didn't seem worth the bother so he waited until he couldn't wait any longer. He tossed back the covers and took the crutch, a wooden one with a sort of rubber hot dog to cushion his armpit, and hobbled to the bathroom. His legs were stiff as unstrung bows. He switched on the light and a haggard invalid squinted back at him from the medicine cabinet mirror. Five putty-colored patches of frostbite streaked his face, two to each cheekbone and one down the bridge of his nose. The peeling skin was like the gray flesh of a cadaver beneath the ruddy flush of surrounding living skin. The phantom's caress had felt so sweet at the time; and her smile — what a strange, knowing thing.

On the way back to bed he stopped at the window and poked his head between the curtains. The few lighted windows along the street were gaseous yellow in the fog. The icicles outside the window had fallen. Old Man Winter had lost his teeth.

Caroline came in and found him like that — in the dark, head stuck through the curtains, flannel shirt hanging open and tucked, sort of, into an old pair of her father's pajama bottoms. "The icicles fell," he said without looking around.

"They came down all along that side a little while ago," she said. "The whole house shook."

He pulled his head out of the curtains and turned around. She was framed in the light of the open doorway. "That must have been what woke me up," he said.

"How do you feel now?"

"Awake."

She did not come closer so he went to her. He leaned on her and pushed the door shut with his crutch. She was dressed for bed.

"You've come to spend the night." He bent to her and nuzzled the open cleft of her robe where modest breasts, each with its prim nipple erect against the softness of the nightgown, parted for him and exposed her heart to his ear. As he listened the beats grew stronger, faster. He breathed in the scent of hyacinth bath powder and fresh linen and the sweet, hot, tallowy smell of woman flesh. He kissed her beating heart.

"Come to bed." He took her by the hand. She resisted. He let go and went back to bed alone and put his feet under the covers. He could barely see her, a paleness in the dark, more aura than flesh and blood. Her eyes were smudges of opacity and he heard her breath in little gusts.

"I can turn on the lamp," he said.

"I prefer the dark."

He patted the mattress beside him. She started round but stopped at the foot of the bed. She bent over. He smelled cedar and heard a muffled jingle, like coins shaken in a sack. She straightened up and glided around the bedside. He held out his arms to her.

"Caroline?"

He knew. He had known the first time he saw her. He knew when they first kissed, and when they made love. And yet it came as a complete surprise.

Clack.

The spring release hit his chin and the steel jaws of the wolf trap shut on his face. The upper jaw broke his nose and bit into his cheekbones, the lower sunk into his throat. He felt no pain, but huge hissing pressure. He could not breathe. The trap had crushed his windpipe and pinned his mouth and his lungs sucked blood. He was drowning.

He tried to pull the jaws apart but she wouldn't let him. She had thrown herself on him with all her strength. They clung together on the bed, fierce and desperate and silent. He managed to stand with her draped over him but the drag chain tripped him and his broken foot gave and they crashed to the floor. He yelled out and there was only a quiet gurgle. He knew he was going to die.

The living organism was in a panic for air. Every cell in his body screamed for it. Her body on top of his grew incredibly heavy. Her great weight pressed into him. He could no longer move his arms and legs. One by one his ribs gave and down she sank into him. She had his heart now. Pressing it. It was fluttery and broken and the instant her wild strong heart touched it, it stopped.

For the first time in his life he knew true silence, as blue and big as a western sky. And through it, like the silver roar of a distant jet, he heard her whisper to him. Before he died he could have sworn she said I love you.